TWO LAMENTABLE TRAGEDIES

THE MALONE SOCIETY
REPRINTS, VOL. 180
2013

PUBLISHED FOR THE MALONE SOCIETY
BY MANCHESTER UNIVERSITY PRESS

Oxford Road, Manchester M13 9NR, UK
and Room 400, 175 Fifth Avenue, New York, NY 10010, USA
www.manchesteruniversitypress.co.uk

Distributed exclusively in the USA by
Palgrave, 175 Fifth Avenue, New York,
NY 10010, USA

Distributed exclusively in Canada by
UBC Press, University of British Columbia, 2029 West Mall,
Vancouver, BC, Canada V6T 1Z2

British Library Cataloguing-in-Publication Data
A catalogue record for this book is available from the British Library

Library of Congress Cataloging-in-Publication Data applied for

ISBN 978-0-7190-9062-2

Typeset by New Leaf Design, Scarborough, North Yorkshire

Printed by Berforts Information Press Ltd, Oxford

This edition of *Two Lamentable Tragedies* was prepared by Chiaki Hanabusa, and checked by E. Giddens. The Society is grateful to the British Library for permission to reproduce their copy of the play (C.34.e.23).

April 2013   E. GIDDENS

INTRODUCTION

The only extant early edition of Robert Yarington's *Two Lamentable Tragedies* was printed in quarto in 1601 (*STC* 26076).[1] The play was not entered in the Registers of the Stationers' Company. Five copies are known to exist; two in the British Library (C.34.e.23, hereafter L1, and C.12.e.21, hereafter L2), one each in the Bodleian Library (Mal.231(9), O), the National Art Library of the Victoria and Albert Museum (Dyce 26. Box 51/3, L⁶), and the Henry E. Huntington Library (K–D 464, HN).[2] Only a limited number of modern editions are available.[3] The present photographic facsimile is a 1:1 reproduction of L1, the best surviving exemplar. O has a number of ink smudges on many of its pages, while the title-page of L⁶ and all the pages of HN were cut out and pasted down on modern paper.

The quarto collates 4°: A–K⁴. The title-page is A1ʳ. The full-title reads 'Two Lamentable | Tragedies. | The one, of the murther of Mai-|*ster* Beech *a Chaundler in* | Thames-streete, and his boye, | done by *Thomas Merry*. | *The other of a young childe mur-*|thered in a Wood by two Ruffins, | *with the consent of his Vnckle.* | By ROB. YARINGTON.'[4] Under the title is a printer's device representing a gilly-flower with two leaves framed by four surrounding borders. It is known that the device, originally Gabriel Simson's, once had his initials 'G S' under the two leaves, but they seem to have been excised, after

---

[1] *A Short-Title Catalogue of Books Printed in England, Scotland, & Ireland and of English Books Printed Abroad 1475–1640*, ed. Alfred W. Pollard and G. R. Redgrave, 2nd edn, rev. W. A. Jackson, F. S. Ferguson, and Katharine F. Pantzer, 3 vols (London, 1976–91), ii. 483.

[2] See *STC*, ii. 483; W. W. Greg, *A Bibliography of the English Printed Drama to the Restoration*, 4 vols (London, 1939–59), i. 292 (no. 182(A)); 'The English Short Title Catalogue (ESTC)', in the British Library Website <http://www.bl.uk/>. The National Art Library has a neatly bound pen-facsimile edition by an unknown transcriber (Dyce 25. F.59): it reproduces the original text page for page, but is sometimes incorrect in transcribing, in particular, the signature and the catchword. The printer's device, ornaments, and ornamental flowers were not transcribed.

[3] Among the modern editions including those in photographic facsimiles are *A Collection of Old English Plays*, ed. A. H. Bullen (London, 4 vols, 1882–5, NS, 3 vols, 1887–90; New York, repr., 1964), iv (1885), 1–97; *Two Lamentable Tragedies by Robert Yarington. 1601*, The Tudor Facsimile Texts, ed. John S. Farmer (Amersham, 1913); *Two Lamentable Tragedies by Robert Yarington*, Old English Drama: Students' Facsimile Edition (Amersham, 1913). Bullen's edition is the only edited text since 1601, but has little commentary. The two facsimile texts reproduce L1, although the latter incorrectly states that it is a reproduction of L2. The most recent but unpublished edition is 'A Critical Old-Spelling Edition of Robert Yarington's *Two Lamentable Tragedies*', ed. Anne Weston Patenaude, 2 vols, unpublished doctoral dissertation, The University of Michigan, 1978. This has so far been the most comprehensive study of the play with full critical and textual introductions, as well as commentary and appendices.

[4] Long-s, ligatures, and swash letters are not reproduced precisely here and elsewhere in the introduction.

it was passed to Richard Read around 1601.[5] W. W. Greg conjectures that the play was printed by Read on the basis of the device.[6] Under the device is the title-page imprint, reading 'LONDON | Printed for *Mathew Lawe*, and are to be solde at | *his shop in Paules Church-yarde neere vnto* | *S. Austines gate, at the signe* | *of the Foxe. 1601*.' The imprint suggests that Matthew Law, widely known as a bookseller, invested capital into the production of the quarto as its publishing bookseller. Law probably procured the manuscript himself, and hired Read as printer. Without entering the title, Law seems to have saved the fee (four pence). Entrance was the requirement for establishing the exclusive rights to republish the play but was not mandatory. Law, however, must have paid the licence fee (six pence) which was mandatory for censorship.[7] A1[v] is blank. At the head of A2[r] is a set of flower ornaments, followed by the head-title, 'Two Tragedies | *in one*.' with another tiny flower ornament.[8] A single linear border is set to divide the head-title from the induction. The induction between Homicide, Avarice, and Truth begins with a centered stage direction. An ornamental initial 'I' is employed at the beginning of the opening speech. The induction ends at TLN 115, the final twenty-seven lines being 'what is in effect a prologue by Truth'.[9] The main text runs from TLN 116 on A3[v] to 2710 on K2[v], after which the conclusion between Truth, Homicide, and Covetousness (i.e. Avarice) follows. The conclusion ends at TLN 2772 on K3[v] with the explicit '*F I N I S. Rob. Yarington.* | Laus Deo.' accompanied by a set of flower ornaments.[10] All the five extant copies lack Leaf K4, which was presumably blank.

In the blank margin of L1's final page, the retail price of the quarto from an unknown age, two shillings six pence, is hand-written as '–o–2–6'. There is an inscription on the final page of L2, which reads '1601.March.28'. This was probably inscribed by the copy's earliest owner as the date of acquisition. If this conjecture is correct, the inscription suggests that the production of the book would have been finished by the end of March at the latest. 'Two Tragedies in one' by 'Robert Yarington' was listed in Francis Kirkman's 'A

[5] This device, 'McKerrow 320 (β)', was used on the title-page of *The Art of Vulgar Arithmetic* (1600, *STC* 14040.7), the book printed by Simson in the year he died. It was passed from Read to George Eld in *c*.1604. Three borders were cut away when it was passed again from Eld to another printer in 1624. For the removal of the initials and the gradual deterioration of the design, see Ronald B. McKerrow, *Printers' & Publishers' Devices in England & Scotland 1485–1640* (London, 1913), pp. 125, 181.

[6] Greg, *Bibliography*, i. 292.

[7] For details of entrance and licence, see Peter W. M. Blayney, 'The Publication of Playbooks'', in *A New History of Early English Drama*, ed. John D. Cox and David Scott Kastan (New York, 1997), pp. 383–422, esp. pp. 398–405.

[8] These flower ornaments were commonly used by contemporary printers. See W. Craig Ferguson, *Valentine Simmes: Printer to Drayton, Shakespeare, Chapman, [...] and other Elizabethans* (Charlottesville, 1968), p. 49 (Flowers 4, 6); Akihiro Yamada, *Thomas Creede: Printer to Shakespeare and his Contemporaries* (Tokyo, 1994), p. 83 (Orn. 23), and his *Peter Short: An Elizabethan Printer* (Mie, 2002), p. 162 (no. 160(b)).

[9] Greg, *Bibliography*, i. 292.

[10] For a brief account of 'explicit', that is, the author's colophon, see Ronald B. McKerrow, *An Introduction to Bibliography for Literary Students* (Oxford, 1927; repr. 1928), p. 95 (n. 1).

True, perfect, and exact Catalogue of all the Comedies, Tragedies, Tragi-Comedies [...] printed and published, till this present year 1661.'[11] The same title appears again in his 1671 Catalogue.[12]

The play is not divided into acts or scenes.[13] All speeches are set in verse, except those in prose spoken by a maid (TLN 782–6) and some lines spoken by two watermen (TLN 1666–9, 1672–3, 1676–1708). Of these prose speeches, a couple of lines are set as if they are verse (1688, 1705), while a verse speech is set as if it is prose for lack of space at the bottom of G1^v (1761–3). Each page normally has thirty-seven text-lines, and the vertical length of the text area excluding the headline and the direction line measures 152–154 millimetres throughout. A2^v, A4^v, and K1^v have only thirty-six lines, while G1^v has thirty-eight.[14] When a stage direction is spaced above and/or below it, the compositor seems to have used two ways of inserting a blank line. A thick lead, or a couple of thinner leads, produces a blank line on A3^r, B1^r, F3^v, H4^r. Elsewhere, only a single thin lead is employed; that is, thirty-six text-lines and two thin leads above and below the direction are filling up the printing area consisting of exactly thirty-seven lines, as C1^r shows for instance. The irregular number of the text-lines, as well as the two ways of leading for stage directions, may reflect the compositor's efforts to catch up with the casting-off points in the manuscript.

Similarly, the compositor took pains to save space and to prevent the text from overflowing the line: he not only avoided indenting the speech prefixes (TLN 130, 482, 502) but curtailed the stage directions to set them neatly in the narrow blank margin (421, 447, 722, 784, 998, 1033, 1184, 1790, 1882, 2137, 2429). He also used tilde (502, 1204, 1882), ampersand (1241), and contraction (868) to squeeze the text.[15] Where he unavoidably had to turn-over a speech, he employed turn-downs, including those stage directions set in two consecutive lines in the right-hand side outer margin (128–9, 344–5, 501, 531–2, 772–3, 786, 793, 869, 1070–1, 1285, 1348, 2637–8). The text was turned-up only once at TLN 1759, where the compositor was unable to turn

---

[11] The play appears on p. 15 of the Catalogue. See Greg, *Bibliography*, iii. 1351. Francis Kirkman, a bookseller in London who was active in 1657–78, was a collector of plays from his boyhood. His catalogue lists 690 plays, 'all the English plays then printed'. See Henry R. Plomer, *A Dictionary of the Booksellers and Printers Who Were at Work in England, Scotland, and Ireland from 1641 to 1667* (London, 1968), pp. 110–11.

[12] This catalogue, in sixteen quarto pages, was bound together and sold with Pierre Corneille's *Nicomede: a Tragi-Comedy* (WING, C6315, 1671). *Two Lamentable Tragedies* is listed on p. 14. For more details of the play's entry in private collections, including Sir John Harrington's completed by 1610, and in the early play-catalogues published in 1656–63, see Greg, *Bibliography*, iii. 1306–57; iv. 1652–62.

[13] Bullen divided the play into five acts consisting of twenty-five scenes, while Patenaude divided it into twenty-eight scenes without act divisions.

[14] The thirty-seventh line of the three underset pages is the direction line where the catchwords are composed. The vertical length, naturally, shrinks to 148.0 mm. At TLN 1763, the final two words of a speech with a period overflowed to the thirty-eighth line, which is *de facto* the direction line. The vertical length measures 155.5 mm.

[15] A tilde is again used at TLN 1761 to set a prose speech. An ampersand appears at TLN 321, but as this is not a full-line, the use of it may have been authorial.

it down due to a full-line speech that immediately follows. He may have taken out a blank line from below the direction to save space (673, 693). On the other hand, the compositor seems to have wasted space elsewhere by dividing a cursory stage direction into two lines (1175–6, 1943–4). He set up, only once, a very short speech in a single line, and left a large blank margin on the right of the speech (348), although he normally filled such an extra space with another short speech in full (147, 169, 171, 792, 1859, 1882, 2073, 2380) or part of a speech that immediately follows (200, 571, 779, 889, 1446). All in all, the above inconsistent textual features ranging from the irregular number of the lines per page to setting prose as if it were verse, taking out a blank line, and saving and wasting space appear to imply that the compositor worked to overcome unsuccessful casting-off. Since at least one of the irregular setting practices occurs in all sheets of the quarto, it would be sound to suggest that the text was set by formes.

The printer's measure is 80–2 millimetres throughout. The variation in line length may have been caused by paper shrinkage and uneven pressure from furniture. The text is mainly set in pica roman fount measuring 82–3 millimetres in twenty lines. The type impression is entirely clear in all five copies, which suggests that the roman types, mostly intact, had not been heavily used before the time of printing the quarto. This coincides with W. Craig Ferguson's analysis of pica roman type that Read owned. Ferguson notes that, after he succeeded to his printing-house from his predecessor in 1601, Read freshly acquired pica roman of the Haultin face in addition to another already existing fount.[16] The fount, however, does contain several damaged types. A lower-case 'e' without the bar appears frequently (e.g. 'hartelie', TLN 170; 'coafer', 216; 'safetie', 650; 'leaue', 653; 'vtter', 704; 'promise', 1028; 'deed', 1204; 'presently', 1477; 'bloodie', 1767; etc.). An upper-case 'C' with the lower part of the stroke seriously cracked appears twice. The recurrence of the majuscule 'C' has been confirmed with definite identification in all five copies ('Come', 450; 'Cease', 1156).[17] Meanwhile, italic type is used for stage directions, speech prefixes, and Latin.[18] Proper names, including allegorical characters and the names originating from the Bible and Greco-Roman myths, are normally set in italic.[19] The names appearing in the stage directions tend to be set in roman, although there are abundant exceptions.[20] There seems to have been no general rule for setting geographical names; to mention only a

[16] W. Craig Ferguson, *Pica Roman Type in Elizabethan England* (Aldershot, 1989), p. 30. For the identification of the face, see pp. 6–7.

[17] For the technical terms of types, here and elsewhere, see Philip Gaskell, 'A Nomenclature for the Letter-forms of Roman Type', *The Library*, 5th series, 29 (1974), 42–51.

[18] The Latin phrase appears only once: '*Ab imo cordis*' ('from the bottom of my heart', TLN 2587).

[19] Also in italic are '*Canibals*' (TLN 87), '*Canniball*' (1323), '*Soldans*' (i.e. sultan's, 624), '*Carbonadoes*' (slices of meat for broiling, 1322), '*Pendragon*' (the name of a hound dog, 1406), 'S. *Andrew*' (patron saint of Scotland, 1969), '*Lauiathan*' (Satan in Hebrew poetry, 2662), etc., while 'the Bull' (457), the name of Merry's tavern, is in roman.

[20] See, for example, '*Enter Trueth.*' (TLN 67), and '*Exit Beech and neigh.*' (203). There are fifteen such directions in all.

few, '*Padua*' (TLN 106, 1068, 1434, 1436, 2005, 2079, 2117, 2282), '*Thames*' (987, 990), '*Lambert Hill*' (991), and '*Paris-garden*' (1196) are italicized, while 'London' (95), 'London walles' (212, 2325), 'Thames' (96), 'Lambert hill' (1710, 2189, 2352, 2367), 'Paris-garden' (1799), 'Bainardes castle' (1603), 'Baynards castle' (1670), and 'Baynardes Castle' (1757) are in roman.[21] In sheets B, E, G, H, and I, only the first three leaves are signed with roman capitals and Arabic numerals, but all four leaves are signed in sheets A, C, D, and F.[22] Textual flaws abound, such as misspelling ('Willl', TLN 151; 'Guesse' instead of 'Guests', 421; 'no boubt', 1768; 'magnamitie', 2000; 'no donbt', 2557; 'grieueuous', 2632), erroneous punctuation marks (use of comma at the end of speech, TLN 129, 286, etc.; comma instead of query, 167, 781, etc.), and mis-located stage directions ('*Exit.*' at a line below, TLN 1613, 1659). The setting of the catchwords is accurate, although hyphenated abbreviations as well as typographical and spelling variations do occur.[23] When a speech head is extremely abbreviated with a numeral, a single word of the following speech usually is composed as the catchword.[24]

Collation of the five extant copies uncovered no press-variants resulting from the stop-press correction. Nor did it reveal any mechanical variants such as the type's shifting, progressive deterioration, or loss. L1 is the cleanest copy of the five in terms of type impression, trimming of the page margins, and aged deterioration of the paper. One may, however, have some difficulties in reading minor details of the text, due to the coarse texture of the contemporary paper with which the quarto was printed. The inferior paper, produced in job-lots and used for such cheap print as play-quartos, does not necessarily have the smooth surface that readers will expect in modern paper. The type impression could become imperfect, incomplete, or even impossible because of the lack of satisfactory flatness on the surface. A rag of paper sticking to the surface often makes the trace of type impression invisible, for instance, in such words as 'to' (TLN 81), 'practise' (88), 'prepare' (89), 'such' (268), 'This' (2666), and 'confesse' (2666). A hole in the paper, often affecting the text printed on the other side as well, renders it hard to read, as for 'best' (412), 'Basiliskes' (603), '*Remooue the*' (1199), 'me downe' (1235), 'I' (1672), 'plot' (2138), 'hart' (2677), and 'riches' (2713).[25] A scratch in the paper produced a

[21] To complicate the matter further, another occurrence of 'Padua' (TLN 1389) is in roman as if it were one of the proper names appearing in a stage direction, while '*Paduans*' (1435) is in italic.

[22] 'I 3.' is signed with a full stop. As leaf K4 is wanting in all five copies, we do not know whether this leaf was signed or not.

[23] Abbreviations are 'Whe-' (A2^r CW) / 'Whether' (the initial word on A2^v); 'Them-' (A2^v CW) / 'Themselues' (A3^r); 'Bro-' (B2^r CW) / 'Brother' (B2^v); 'With-' (C1^v CW) / 'Within' (C2^r); 'There-' (D4^v CW) / 'Therefore' (E1^r); 'Per-' (G2^v CW) / 'Perchance' (G3^r); '*Loney.*' (G3^r CW) / '*Lon.*' (G3^v); 'Vn-' (K1^r CW) / 'Vngratefulnesse' (K1^v). Typographical and spelling variations are '*1.Wat.*' (G1^v CW) / '*1.VVat.*' (G2^r); '*Alen.*' (H1^r CW) / '*Allen.*' (H1^v).

[24] See '*2.* This' (D3^r CW) and '*2.m.*But' (E3^v CW). The only exception to this practice is '*1.Wat.*' (G1^v CW).

[25] The holes on B3^v (2×5 millimetres) and E2^r–E2^v (2×2 millimetres) are two of the largest of all.

bumpy surface, thereby making some spellings illegible such as 'make' (444), 'his' (1146), 'barbarous' (1208), 'he' (1325), 'extremities' (1514), 'Amongst' (1809), 'seene' (2116), 'seemes' (2177), 'arrest' (2273), and 'consumate' (2612). A stain or smudge on the paper prevented a clear type impression of 'take' (236) and 'dye,' (with comma, 2771). Locally heavy or weak pressure from the press on a couple of types, the reason for which is hard to decipher but may somehow relate to the peculiar setting of the types, produced an inked space (238, 2497), show-through of an upper-case 'A' on the right-hand side margin (563), and a normal but extremely weak impression ('sonne', 2441).[26] Either erroneous or weak spacing caused such irregular readings as 'sau e you' (1036), 'Which n ature' (1321), 'm y brother' (1881), and 'Na y did' (2452).

The author seems to have had the correct knowledge as to the locution of the stage directions as well as their refined use, for he quite rightly used the conventional theatrical language such as *'solus'* (TLN 18, 388, etc.), *'To the people'* (271, 290, etc.), *'Exeunt omnes: manet [...]'* (1048, 1571, etc.), *'[...] two Murtherers booted.'* (1058), or *'A hunt within.'* (1388). He was definitely aware of inserting the 'early' entry direction assigned in advance of the character's initial speech. For example, the entry direction for Avarice is written three lines earlier than he actually enters (TLN 41). *'Enter* Beech *and a friend.'* (125) is located four lines earlier than their conversation begins. There exist, however, long, descriptive directions which verbally illustrate the stage actions but cannot help inducing doubts whether they could actually be performed as instructed, for instance, *'Then being in the vpper Rome* Merry *strikes him in the head fifteene times.'* (463–4), and *'When the boy goeth into the shoppe* Merrie *striketh six blowes on his head & With the seauenth leaues the hammer sticking in his head, the boy groaning must be heard by a maide who must crye to her maister.* Merrie *flieth.'* (752–6). It seems dubious whether the player of Merry struck Beech exactly *'fifteene times'*, or that he gave the boy's head *'six blowes [...] & With the seauenth leaues the hammer sticking in his head'*. These somewhat awkward directions must have originated from the author's creative imagination for staging.

The bookkeeper may have hoped to avoid missing or erroneous stage directions, unless the precise action was predicted by surrounding speeches. Merry's speech 'Hoe *Rachell*, bring my cloake, [...]' (TLN 418) supplies the necessary information for Rachel, despite the absence of her entry direction. Similarly, Merry's speech ordering Rachel to 'Go downe and see, [...]' (706) compensates for the lack of Rachel's exit direction. More serious absent directions, however, occur throughout the play. For example, Fallerio's speech, 'If it were seald, I would you both were dead.' (280), clearly had to accompany the direction *'To the people.'*, for it must never have been heard by anyone

---

[26] The inked space and the show-through can be seen in all the five copies, while the weak impression is detectable in L1 alone.

else.[27] The direction should have been supplied where Merry shows his hideous intent to kill Beech who is just in front him (452–4), and where Fallerio tells himself that his son is disguised (2443–4). Likewise, '*Enter* Merry *and* Rachell.' (907) had to be accompanied by '*aloft*' or '*above*', for the brother and sister clearly appear on the upper stage. There are incorrect speech prefixes that the bookkeeper would not allow to stand. The relenting murderer is assigned '*1.mur.*' instead of the correct '*2.mur.*' (1379), and the beastly murderer who killed Pertillo has '*2.mur.*' (1387) when '*1.mur.*' is correct. Along with the lack or incorrectness of the stage directions and imprecise speech prefixes above, absence of the bookkeeper's typical direction to make a particular character '*ready*' in advance of the actual entrance, or of his careful note for preparation of large properties such as a bed,[28] which in fact is necessary at TLN 226, suggests collectively that the copy-text was not a theatrical manuscript but authorial in origin.

The text is, as a matter of fact, full of the author's visually imaginative speeches and actions, while some of his stage requirements appear difficult to carry out. For example, the scene where the salter's man was sent knocking at doors to search for a maid who bought the bag in which part of Beech's body was found requires four different onstage locations simultaneously, namely, Looney's house, two private houses, and Merry's shop. The three neighbours, who gather in front of Looney's house and knock on the door (1716–17), discuss the current situation and depart for their search by knocking on the door of one of the two neighbouring houses, before they finally reach Merry's tavern (1866–73). Clearly, the progress of the successive actions requires a wide stage. In view of relatively high flexibility allowed for the Elizabethan plays, one should not always expect too realistic staging of every minor detail including the upper space and the stage doors. However, the clumsy staging such as bringing forth Winchester in his sick-chair '*with a hammer | sticking in his head*' (1007–8), or gathering Beech's severed head, legs, and body, all dummy, at one place to hear Looney propose that 'Lay them together see if they can make, | Among them all a sound and solid man.' (1793–4) must have been difficult to perform: the author's magnitude of imagination slipped beyond theatricality. These actions were, it seems, not amended by the bookkeeper's professional insights.

The text as it stands has potential difficulties in informing the audience appropriately of the characters' names. In Pandino and Armenia's death-bed scene, the first reference to the personal name is to that of Pertillo (TLN 304),

[27] This direction means 'either *aside* or "to the playgoer" (as with a choric speech)'. See Alan C. Dessen and Leslie Thomson, *A Dictionary of Stage Directions in English Drama, 1580–1642* (Cambridge, 1999), p. 161.

[28] See William B. Long, ' "A bed / for woodstock": A Warning for the Unwary', *Medieval & Renaissance Drama in England*, 2 (1985), 91–118. The direction such as '*ready*' and the bookkeeper's note for large properties are called 'the warning direction', that is, 'a direction that advises the prompter of an entrance, a prop, or a sound [...] required somewhat later in performance'. See Paul Werstine, *Early Modern Playhouse Manuscripts and the Editing of Shakespeare* (Cambridge, 2013), p. 209.

but then seventy-nine lines of conversation have already passed. The sick Pandino and Armenia's names are disclosed a further fifty-seven lines below (361), while there is no information at all on Fallerio and Sostrata's names in this scene; the audience is given at the opening of the scene only their relationship to Pandino and Armenia as 'Brother and sister' (229). It certainly is odd that the name of one of the main characters of the play, Fallerio, is kept unmentioned throughout the entire scene. The similar phenomenon occurs again at the wood scene where the Duke of Padua and his lords return from hunting and meet Allenso. The Duke enters (1389) but is never called by his title, nor are any of his lords, Turqualo, Vesuvio, and Albert addressed by their names, from their first entrance to the end of the scene (1578). Reference to the Duke occurs for the first time further down the text at TLN 2079.

A couple of stage directions are so exceptional as to violate the conventional locution for directions. The playwright uses '*Exit vp.*' twice (TLN 478, 495); in one scene, Rachel brings up a light for Merry and Beech to the upper stage and, in the other, Harry Williams goes up to see what has been committed by Merry. The stage direction here would, normally, have been either '*Go vp*' or '*Go aloft*'. The rare use of the locution is immediately demonstrated by 'Literature Online' database <http://lion.chadwyck.co.uk>. Of all dramatic texts (1558–1660) recorded in the database, the play is the sole example in which the direction '*Exit vp.*' is used. Also exceptional is a combination of two directions in the final execution scene, which read '*Turne of[f] the Lather:* Rachel *shrinketh.*' (TLN 2676). A ladder, one of the popular stage props (e.g. a scaling ladder, a ladder of cords, etc.), appears in a total of twenty-one plays. '*Turne of[f] the Lather*', however, is a quite exceptional phrase. According to the database, the play is the only source of this direction.[29] The direction is so unfamiliar that the precise onstage performance of 'turning off the ladder' is as yet unexplained. Anne Weston Patenaude remarks on this point that 'The direction is unclear whether Merry turns himself [jumps] off the ladder or gallows structure, or whether he is "aided" by the Officer or Hangman'.[30] 'Rachel *shrinketh* ' is a rare direction, too.[31] The 'literary' direction that

---

[29] For a variant phrase used for hanging, see, for example, 'fling him of[f] ye lader', in John Pikering's *Horestes* (1567, *STC* 19917, D2^r) and 'He [Hangman] turnes him off', in Thomas Kyd's *The Spanish Tragedy* (1592, *STC* 15086, F3^v).

[30] Patenaude, 'Critical Old-Spelling Edition', p. 328. John H. Astington conjectures that gallows scenes in contemporary plays were performed with ropes, pulleys, and body harness attached to the actor to be 'hanged' safely, in his 'Gallows Scenes on the Elizabethan Stage', *Theatre Notebook*, 37 (1983), 3–9. The editors of the most recent edition of *The Spanish Tragedy* accept his view and infer that 'the Hangman may bring in a ladder, stool or box besides the rope', in *The Spanish Tragedy*, Arden Early Modern Drama, ed. Clara Calvo and Jesús Tronch (London, 2013), p. 213. In *Two Lamentable Tragedies*, the Hangman enters only with '*a lather*' (TLN 2616).

[31] Patenaude is silent as to this fact in her 'Critical Old-Spelling Edition', so are Dessen and Thomson in their *Dictionary of Stage Directions* and in their website with the same title <http://www.sddictionary.com/index.html>.

makes someone 'shrink' on the stage is employed in only three contemporary plays.[32]

On the basis of the requirement of a sufficiently large and wide stage, some awkward and comical staging effects, a lack of expository structure to inform the audience of personal names, and the use of extremely rare and exceptional locutions for the stage directions, two observations can be made: one is that the author may have had less theatrical experience than his colleagues amongst professional playwrights; the other is that the play as it stands was never performed. As a matter of fact, the play is Yarington's only work that survives, and the title-page has no mention of a dramatic company staging it. Yarington had a good command of theatrical language, as I mentioned above, but he probably may have given up his career before he became full-fledged. The text was probably written soon after Merry's murder case occurred, but, for the reasons discussed above, the play may never have reached the stage. The script was then dismissed, and left unattended by any dramatic company, until the publisher somehow procured the manuscript and decided to put it to print in 1601. The text, full of scandalous and tragic plots skilfully woven into a single story, might have been seen as better for a reading public than a theatrical audience.

As to the style of the text, Robert Adger Law called attention to verbal parallels detected in *King Leir* and *Richard III*.[33] He first pointed out in 1910 that 'Yarington took the words from the earlier play', referring to 'Ah, do not so disconsolate your selfe', identical between *Two Lamentable Tragedies* (TLN 919) and *Leir*.[34] He not only listed half a dozen such parallels from *Leir* but detected similar phrases between *Two Lamentable Tragedies* and *Richard III*, such as 'Thou raw-bonde lumpe of foule deformitie.' (TLN 1530) and 'Blush blush thou lumpe of foule deformity' in *Richard III*.[35] He concluded that Yarington borrowed the phrases from the two earlier plays. Law refined his discussion in 1927 by submitting a list of parallel incidents occurring both in *Two Lamentable Tragedies* and *Richard III* to conclude that 'Yarington, an immature and unimaginative writer, borrowed material for his play wholesale from contemporary writers or playwrights'.[36] The stylistic analysis of the play in terms of parallels or phrases borrowed from other dramatic texts has remained stagnant since Law. In 2006, MacD. P. Jackson

---

[32] The other two plays are Thomas Dekker's *Troia-Nova Triumphans* (1612, *STC* 6530), and Anthony Munday's *Fedele and Fortunio* (1585, *STC* 19447).

[33] *Leir* (*STC* 15343), printed in 1605, had been entered on 14 May 1594. *Richard III* (*STC* 22314), printed in 1597, had probably been performed in 1592. See Greg, *Bibliography*, i. 230 (no. 142 (a)), 337 (no. 213(A)); *The Tragedy of King Richard III*, ed. John Jowett (Oxford, 2000), p. 8.

[34] See Robert Adger Law, 'Yarington's *Two Lamentable Tragedies*', *Modern Language Review*, 5 (1910), 167–77, esp. pp. 173–7, and *The History of King Leir 1605*, ed. W. W. Greg, Malone Society Reprint (Oxford, 1907), TLN 866, respectively.

[35] *Richard the Third 1597*, ed. W. W. Greg, Shakespeare Quarto Facsimiles No. 12 (Oxford, 1959), I. ii. 57.

[36] Robert Adger Law, 'Further Notes on "Two Lamentable Tragedies"', *Notes and Queries*, 153 (1927), 93–4, esp. p. 94.

conducted statistical research on the quarrel scene in *Arden of Faversham*, and discovered that the scene shared a number of phrases with dozens of contemporary dramas including Shakespeare's plays, and that Yarington was second after Shakespeare.[37] His research on the scene's authorship, focusing on compound adjectives, uncovered that Yarington was 'ridiculously partial to compound adjectives, even of the kinds characteristic of Shakespeare'. He finally dismissed the possibility that Yarington wrote part of *Arden*, due to his 'incoherence, awkward construction, and naïve psychology' in *Two Lamentable Tragedies*.[38] More recently, Marcus Dahl has discovered as many as forty parallel phrases detected exclusively in the play and *Leir*, and thirty more phrases shared by more than three plays.[39] Yarington's preference for compound adjectives has to be recognized in its own right as his finger print, and Yarington's individual style awaits more rigorous research in relation to that of Shakespeare. These stylistic approaches would be a clue to enhance future analysis of the dramatist who has only a single surviving play.

The headline of the quarto, set in larger roman type, first appears on A2^v and reads 'Two Tragedies in one.' on both recto and verso pages. Spelling variants do not occur, nor do damaged types that can clearly be identified exist. As both features are an indispensable tool for identifying the headline, the lack of spelling variations and the absence of the typographical evidence in satisfactory quantity have, unfortunately, made the complete identification of separate running-titles invalid. Nevertheless, there is reason to believe that two sets of the headlines, consisting of eight running-titles, were probably used to print the quarto.[40] Of all the running-titles, two are clearly identifiable. One has a lower-case 'g' (of 'Tragedies') with a crack in its tail as well as a black-letter period at the end. This running-title regularly appears in the outer forme throughout, and always reappears on '3^r' pages of all sheets but B, where it appears on B1^r, presumably accidentally. The other is a bent headline, where the type lineage of 'wo Tragedies' looks slightly warped upwards. This headline regularly appears in the inner forme throughout, and reappears on '2^r' pages of all sheets but A and F: in the inner forme of sheet A, as only two headlines were necessary on A3^v and A4^r, with the regular arrangement of four headlines not being established yet, the warped headline appears on A3^v. Later on, it reappears on F4^r, possibly accidentally again. The fact that the

[37] MacDonald P. Jackson, 'Shakespeare and the Quarrel Scene in *Arden of Faversham*', *Shakespeare Quarterly*, 57 (2006), 249–93, esp. p. 259.

[38] MacD. P. Jackson, 'Compound Adjectives in *Arden of Faversham*', *Notes and Queries*, 53 (2006), 51–5, esp. p. 54. The citation by Jackson here originates from Henry Hitch Adams, *English Domestic or Homiletic Tragedy 1575 to 1642* (New York, 1943), p. 108.

[39] Private correspondence. I am grateful to Dr Marcus Dahl, Lecturer in Authorship Studies, University of London, for his kindness in providing me with all his statistics on the authorship question of the play.

[40] This 'set of the headlines' is part of 'a skeleton forme' accompanied by wooden furniture and quoins for locking up the four pages in the case of quarto.

two headlines almost always reappear on an apparently fixed page both in the outer and inner formes in sheets A–K suggests that each of the two headlines is one each of four headlines making up a single 'set', and that the two sets, X and Y, were employed for the entire book. That is to say, set X, including the headline with a cracked 'g' and a black-letter period, was employed regularly in the outer forme, while set Y containing a warped headline was used in the inner forme. Although the headline identification is far from complete with six headlines unidentified, there is a sound basis on which to believe that the quarto was printed with two sets of the headlines throughout.

Examination of the watermarks has been carried out in all the surviving copies. The watermark wired in the middle space at the left-hand side of a paper mould, along with the countermark (if it exists) at the right, is, in the quarto format, regularly visible at the narrow gutter of the bound book; only an unbound copy would provide the mark's entire image. In this quarto, the watermarks are not always visible enough to identify their designs. Of the fifty sheets in the five extant copies (ten sheets per copy, from A to K), the watermarks were detected in thirty-six sheets. The marks were invisible in eleven sheets, while they were visible but unidentifiable in three sheets because of the extremely small visible parts of the design. The search for the watermark has revealed, although incompletely, that at least four kinds of watermarks appear repeatedly in the paper used for the printing of the book. The four designs of the watermark consist of 'Pot' (with the initials 'I B', hereafter P), 'Hand-and-Star' (R), and 'Hand' (S); the remaining mark is of an indeterminate image (Q). It is widely known that, before 1700, the paper used in London was generally imported from the Continent, and that designs of the watermark, such as 'Pot', 'Hand-and-Star', and 'Hand', were all in full favour in the French paper mills.[41] It seems certain that the three kinds of paper used for the extant copies were of French origin. Unfortunately, only one of the three watermarks can be identified in the standard reference sources.[42] P appears to be identical with what Thomas L. Gravell identified as 'POT.106.1' in his 'Watermark Archive'.[43] Gravell detected P in one of the manuscript papers of

[41] See Edward Heawood, *Watermarks Mainly of the 17th and 18th Centuries* (Hilversum, 1950; repr. 1957), pp. 24, 26. 'Hand-and-Star' especially points to French origins, such as Normandy and other northern and central regions (p. 26).

[42] The reference books include C. M. Briquet, *Les Filigranes: Dictionnaire Historique Des arques Du Papier Dès Leur Apparition Vers 1282 Jusqu'en 1600*, 4 vols (Geneva: [n. pub.], 1907; repr. New York, 1966); W. A. Churchill, *Watermarks in Paper in Holland, England, France, etc., in the XVII and XVIII Centuries and Their Interconnection* (Amsterdam, 1935); Heawood, *Watermarks*; Ferguson, *Valentine Simmes*; J. S. G. Simmons and B. J. van Ginneken-van de Kasteele, eds, *Likhachev's Watermarks*, 2 vols (Amsterdam, 1994). Searchable digital databases include David L. Gants's 'A Digital Catalogue of Watermarks and Type Ornaments Used by William Stansby in the Printing of The Workes of Beniamin Jonson (London: 1616)' <http://www2.iath.virginia.edu/gants/>; 'The Watermark Database of the Dutch University Institute for Art History' <http://www.wm-portal.net/niki/index.php>.

[43] 'The Thomas L. Gravell Watermark Archive' <http://www.gravell.org/>, accessed on 20 May 2012. This archive reproduces more than two thousand digital images Gravell collected.

the Bagot family of Blithfield, Staffordshire, which was written in 1598, three years before the quarto was printed.

No further information on the paper has turned up in the present research, but the analysis of the four watermarks provides the basis, though not definitive, on which to infer the order in which the paper was used in the quarto's printing process. P appears regularly in sheet A of the five copies; Q is discernible in all sheets B–E; R exists in sheets F–G of L1, O, and L⁶; and S is observed in sheets H–K of L2, L⁶, and HN.[44] The corollary would be that, as far as we can deduce from the evidence supplied by the five copies, sheet A was printed with the paper marked with P exclusively, and that the paper stock may have been used up at the end of its printing. Sheets B–E probably were printed with the paper marked with Q, and, presumably, the paper stock had been exhausted before the printing of sheet F began. Likewise, it may be possible to assume that sheets F–G were machined with the paper marked with R exclusively, while sheets H–K with the paper marked with S alone. Although it is impossible to provide a decisive conclusion until there has been more extensive paper research of Richard Read's printing-house in and around 1601,[45] the current watermark research suggests, at least, that the quarto was printed with four kinds of French paper; the stock of the paper marked with Q was probably the largest, for it was used for the printing of four sheets, B–E; the paper marked with S may have formed the second largest stock, for it was consumed during the printing of three sheets, H–K. If we were to be allowed to reach any kind of conclusion from only the five surviving exemplars, it would be of interest that each of the four paper stocks was used up successively for the production of a single or more sheet(s); that is to say, the single stock was evidently exhausted per sheet or group of sheets.

Compositor identification has been carried out with the help of such distinguishing markers as spacing and spelling habits. It is widely known that the Elizabethan compositor could control minor typographical details, such as spacing, with some degree of freedom. As a result, the compositor could 'express his typographical personality despite the constraints his text laid upon him'. While the compositor's spelling was not infrequently affected by that of the copy, his habitual spacing offers 'psychomechanical' evidence that can scarcely reflect the influence of copy.[46] Hence pyschomechanical evidence, that is, spacing and unspacing of the final colon (and semicolon) and of

[44] Not all the watermarks are visible here; the mark is invisible in sheets F of L1, G of L⁶, H of HN, and K of L2.

[45] According to Adrian Weiss, research on paper and the paper stock has to be carried out 'in the context of the ideal of examining the papers in every book printed during the proximate period'. See his 'Watermark Evidence and Inference: New Style Dates of Edmund Spenser's *Complaints* and *Daphnaida*', *Studies in Bibliography*, 52 (1999 [2000]), 129–54, esp. p. 133.

[46] See T. H. Howard-Hill, 'New Light on Compositor E of the Shakespeare First Folio', *The Library*, 6th series, 2 (1980), 156–78, esp. pp. 163–4, and his 'The Compositors of Shakespeare's Folio Comedies', *Studies in Bibliography*, 26 (1973), 61–106, esp. p. 65, respectively.

queries after the final word at the end of the unjustified lines,[47] provides the more reliable identifying basis than spelling. The occurrence of a number of spellings used with high frequency has been counted, and the compositor's spelling habits have been employed as secondary, supporting evidence to identify the compositor page by page.

Of seventy-six pages where the main text is printed, colon, semicolon, and question mark at the end of short lines are variously spaced; colon and semicolon are, more often than not, spaced in twenty-four pages, while unspaced colon and semicolon are more frequently observed in forty-one pages (their numbers are even in eleven pages). The final colon and semicolon are almost always unspaced (10 spaced/63 unspaced) in eighteen pages in sheets A–B and the outer forme of sheet C (hereafter C(o)), while in fifty-eight pages in the inner forme of sheet C (hereafter C(i)) and in sheets D–K one to three pages per forme are spaced and the rest of pages in the forme were unspaced (81/102). For example, only one colon is spaced at TLN 88 in all six pages in sheet A (1/34), while in I2^v, I3^v, and I4^r, colon and semicolon are more often spaced (13/6), but in I1^r, I1^v, I2^r, I3^r, and I4^v, the marks are normally unspaced (1/16). The fact suggests that there were at least two compositors at work, namely, spacing compositor (S) and unspacing compositor (U).

The composition seems to have proceeded in two distinct stages. The first five formes in sheets A–B and C(o) were composed by U alone, as is indicated by the fact that 86.3 per cent of colons and semicolons are unspaced. Although the numbers of (un)spaced marks are even on B1^v (1 spaced/1 unspaced) and C1^r (1/1), one may well suppose that the two spaced marks would have been either accidental or of human error. We are uncertain as to C2^v (0/0) for lack of evidence. From C(i) to the end of the text on K3^v, Compositor S sporadically joined U for help on at least one page per forme (but not more than three). S spaced in twenty-four pages (59/19), while U unspaced in twenty-six pages (12/83). The numbers are even in eight pages in C(i) and sheets D–K, which we leave unidentified for a moment.

Analysis of the (un)spaced question marks is of no avail. The frequency of appearance is relatively low in comparison with colon and semicolon, with even numbers of spaced and unspaced queries (33/33). Consequently, their occurrences provide no clear trace; the compositors may have spaced them indifferently without any characteristic pattern.

Spelling analysis has been conducted with the use of the electronic text of the play in 'Literature Online'. High frequency words, such as do/doe, hart/heart, here/heere, Merry/Merrie, murther/murder, poore/poor/pore, why/whie, and young/yong have been counted page by page. The spelling variation do/doe, with the highest frequency of all, 125 times (do 90/doe 35), serves best, as supporting evidence, to reinforce the reliability of a division of

---

[47] As the text approaches to the end of the line, the compositor tends to avoid turn-overs, which may involve resetting of the line immediately above or cause him extra work in the line below. In the circumstances, he was deterred from his normal habit and forced to unspace the punctuation marks in all such cases.

labour. From the rest of the spellings, it is hard to distinguish a pattern, for both S and U almost always tend to choose the single spelling (here 26/heere 8, Merry 30/Merrie 8, murther 20/murder 0, poore 19/poor 0/pore 0, why 53/whie 4, and young 15/yong 1). Alternatively, they employ various spellings so randomly without habitual tendencies that a clear pattern never stands out (hart 33/heart 23). Accuracy of the two compositors' division was, therefore, checked against doe/do variation, with the result that the spacing compositor S almost always preferred 'do' to 'doe' (23/1), while U was indifferent to do/doe variation (47/32). As supporting evidence, the clear distinction of their spelling habits provides the basis on which to believe that the workmen's division identified by the spacing evidence above is reliable. Of a total of eleven pages in which the numbers of (un)spaced colon and semicolon are even or none, 'do' spelling prevails in ten pages (19/1) and in a single page both 'do' and 'doe' occur once each. One may conclude that the ten pages were likely to have been set by Compositor S, which is in fact not unreasonable, but it is safer not to identify those pages, for the indifferent Compositor U prefers 'do' to 'doe' approximately half the time. Of thirty punctuation errors, U was responsible for twenty-five, while S was for five. Likewise, U committed eight misspellings, but S had only three. In view of these composing techniques, S perhaps was a superior workman to U.

To conclude, on the basis of spacing evidence, with a reasonable support by a single spelling preference, the compositor identification has led to the conclusion that the text was set by two compositors. Compositor U set sheets A–B and C(o) plus twenty-six pages in C(i) and sheets D–K (C1^v, C4^r, D3^v, D4^r, D4^v, E3^r, E3^v, F3^r, F3^v, F4^v, G1^v, G2^r, G3^r, G4^v, H2^r, H2^v, H3^r, I1^r, I1^v, I2^r, I3^r, I4^v, K1^r, K1^v, K2^r, and K3^r). Compositor S worked on twenty-four pages in C(i) and sheets D–K (C2^r, D1^r, D1^v, D3^r, E1^v, E2^v, E4^r, E4^v, F1^v, F2^r, F2^v, G1^r, G2^v, G3^v, G4^r, H1^r, H1^v, H3^r, H4^v, I2^v, I3^v, I4^r, K2^v, and K3^v). Eleven pages where the spacing and unspacing evidence is weak or none, namely, B1^v (1/1), C1^r (1/1), C2^v (0/0), C3^v (1/1), D2^r (1/1), D2^v (2/2), E1^r (2/2), E2^r (0/0), F1^r (1/1), F4^r (1/1), and H4^r (2/2), are left unidentified. Of the entire text of the play, Compositor U set a total of forty-one pages (53.9 per cent) as against Compositor S's twenty-four (31.6 per cent), with eleven pages (14.5 per cent) left unidentified for lack of evidence.

*

Richard Read had only a brief career as printer in London.[48] He was apprenticed to Richard Jugge, but, as Jugge died in 1577,[49] he was freed by his wife

---

[48] For Read's career as printer, see *A Dictionary of Printers and Booksellers in England, Scotland and Ireland, and of Foreign Printers of English Books 1557–1640*, ed. Ronald B. McKerrow (London, 1910), p. 225; *STC*, iii. 143.

[49] The will of Richard Jugge survives, in which he requests that 'each of my two apprentices William White and Richard Reade shall have twentie shillings a pece at the ende of their prentishipps'. See Henry R. Plomer, *Abstracts from the Wills of English Printers and Stationers, from 1492 to 1630* (London, 1903), p. 24.

Johan Jugge on 18 January 1580.[50] Read definitely had an apprentice at the end of 1584, but his earliest record of entrance appeared in the Registers of the Stationers' Company on 12 May 1601.[51] As far as we know from the extant books, he was an active printer only in 1601–3; the book he first printed was issued in 1601, and his name never reappeared in any of the title-page imprints nor elsewhere after 1604. Three years after his freedom, Gabriel Simson and William White were freed on 10 April 1583 by Mistress Jugge,[52] and Simson and White were given Jugge's printing materials. After their partnership broke up in 1596, Simson retained Jugge's printing materials.[53] After Simson's death (dated before 11 August 1600), and when Read married Simson's widow, Frances, in 1601, Read retained Simson's printing materials, including his device 'McKerrow 320 (β)'. Read became a master printer in the following year.[54] The fact that Frances married George Eld in 1604 suggests that Read may have died between 1603–4.

Of the forty-one items recorded to have been printed by Read in the *STC* and 'ESTC' <http://estc.bl.uk/>, none of them shows his full name in the title-page imprint; only his initials, 'R.R.', were printed in seven books. He resided in Fleet Lane in 1601–2, as, in two of the seven instances, the imprint describes him 'dwelling in Fleete Lane (or Fleet-lane)'.[55] He was evidently not a printer/publisher, but a hired printer. Almost all his books were printed under contract with London publishers. The only exceptions were the two books above with his address printed in the imprint; they were entered by himself and do not contain the publisher's name on the title-page. Read had contracts with a number of publisher/booksellers, including Thomas Pavier, J. Harrison [2] (four items each), Matthew Law, E. Blount, Cuthbert Burby, Thomas Thorpe, G. Potter (three items each), and so on. He shared the printing of books in four instances, with Simon Stafford, Edward Allde, Thomas Creede, and so on.[56] His yearly output was ten items (1601), nine items (1602), and twenty-two items (1603), with religious books accounting for 53.7 per cent (twenty-two items) and literary works for 26.8 per cent (eleven) of his entire output. Literary books worth noting include Ben Jonson's *Cynthia's Revels* (1601, *STC* 14773), *True Chronicle History of Thomas Lord Cromwell* by W. S. (1602, *STC* 21532), and Samuel Daniel's *Congratulatory to the King's Majesty* (1603, *STC* 6260). Read also printed books on medicine and current

[50] See Edward Arber, *A Transcript of the Registers of the Company of Stationers of London, 1554–1640 A.D.*, 5 vols (London and Birmingham, 1875–94), ii. 681.

[51] Arber, *Transcript*, ii. 130, and iii. 184, respectively.   [52] Arber, *Transcript*, ii. 688.

[53] McKerrow, *Dictionary*, pp. 246–7; *STC*, iii. 155, 182. White acquired the printing materials of Richard Jones, and printed *Love's Labour's Lost* in 1598, and in 1600 the second quarto of *3 Henry VI*.

[54] Arber, *Transcript*, iii. 703.

[55] One is John Carpenter's *Contemplations for the Institution of Children* (1601, *STC* 4662, entered on 18 Oct. 1601), and the other is Nicholas Bourman's *An Epitaph ... of Lady Mary Ramsey* (1602, *STC* 3415, entered on 24 Feb. 1602).

[56] Read shared the printing of Sir John Hayward's *An Answer ... Concerning Succession* (1603, *STC* 12988) with as many as five other printers, namely, Richard Bradock, Peter Short, Thomas East, Richard Field, and J. Harrison [3].

news, both domestic and foreign, as well as history, such as Francis Bacon's *A Brief Discourse, Touching the Happy Union of the Kingdoms of England and Scotland* (1603, *STC* 1117).

Matthew Law took the role of the publisher/bookseller for *Two Lamentable Tragedies*, as mentioned above, and was active as such during 1595–1629.[57] He was originally freed from the Drapers' Company on 26 June 1579. Two extant books, printed in 1595 and 1596, were evidently published by him while he was a draper.[58] On 3 June 1600, he was transferred to the Stationers' Company,[59] and, subsequently, his first entrance was recorded on 4 September 1600.[60] According to the title-page imprint of one of his books published in 1601, his bookshop seems to have been located first 'in Paules Church-yard neere Watling-streete'.[61] But he apparently moved by the time Read printed *Two Lamentable Tragedies* for him, and Law set up his bookshop near 'S. Austines [Augustine's] gate' with the sign of the Fox, as the quarto's imprint indicates.[62] He kept this shop until the end of his career.[63] His connection with Read did not last long due to Read's brief career, with the result that they printed and published only two other books together between 1601–2.[64] From 1613, Law kept selling books printed by Cantrell Legge, the printer of Cambridge University; of ten *STC* items, six titles were Richard Kilby's books on theology. They continued their transactions for five years until 1618. After Law published his final book in 1629, he seems to have died, for his will was proved on 26 November 1629.

The *STC* lists ninety-six items that Law was involved in selling and/or publishing throughout his career in 1595–1629. An analysis of the number of items that he sold illustrates that his bookshop flourished in the middle phase of his business; the output for every five years was three (1595–1600), twenty-three (1601–5), twenty-four (1606–10), nineteen (1611–15), fourteen (1616–20), ten (1621–5), and three (1626–9). Of the ninety-six items, religious books account for 64.6 per cent (sixty-two items), followed by literature, which is 24.0 per cent (twenty-three items). In his early career, from 1595 to 1603, Law was involved in the publication of a variety of books on his-

---

[57] For Law's career as bookseller, see McKerrow, *Dictionary*, pp. 169–70; *STC*, iii. 103.

[58] One is *Emaricdulfe, Sonnets Written by E.C. Esquire* ('At London: Printed [by John Orwin] for Matthew Law, 1595.', *STC* 4268), and the other is anonymous *Rome's Monarchy* ('At London: Printed by the widdow Orwin for Matthew Lawe, 1596.', *STC* 21296).

[59] Law was admitted as a freeman of the Company, along with ten other ex-drapers including Thomas Pavier. See Arber, *Transcript*, ii. 725.

[60] Then Law entered '*A hand Diall* in one she[e]te', and paid six pence. See Arber, *Transcript*, iii. 171.

[61] The book is William Barlow's *Sermon Preached at Paul's Cross* (1601, *STC* 1454).

[62] For the location of St Augustine's Gate, see Peter W. M. Blayney, *The Bookshops in Paul's Cross Churchyard* (London, 1990), p. 3 (a map on the facing page).

[63] The only exception is the imprint of Thomas Playfere's *The Whole Sermons* (1623, *STC* 20003), where the address reads, 'Pauls Churchyard, at the signe of the Rose, neere Saint Augustines Gate'. This probably was an error, for the Rose was the sign used by Henry Fetherstone, bookseller, in 1609–26 (*STC*, iii. 238).

[64] The two books are Barlow's *Sermon* (1601, *STC* 1454) and an anonymous news pamphlet entitled *A Dialogue and Complaint Made vpon the Siedge of Oastend* (1602, *STC* 18892).

tory, news, education, and medicine. From 1604, however, he seems to have formed his bookselling business policy and sold books solely in two specific areas; almost all books that he sold were either of a religious or literary nature. He most often sold theological tracts and sermons written and preached by William Barlow, bishop of Lincoln (fourteen items) between 1601–9. Later on, from 1607 to 1623, seven religious items by Richard Kilby, Hebraist, and five by Thomas Playfere, clergyman of the Church of England, were offered for sale at his bookshop.

As to literary books, Law's persistent interest in playbooks throughout his career is worth mentioning. Besides a few exceptions, such as Thomas Middleton and Thomas Dekker's pamphlet describing the outbreak of bubonic plague in May 1603 and verses written by minor poets, the rest of the literary books sold at his bookshop were all dramatic texts. He repeatedly published a small number of plays, and this was made possible by establishing their 'copy-right' through their entry into the Registers. Law entered a total of twenty-five titles from 1600 to 1624. Of these, the most noteworthy entry would be that of William Shakespeare's *Richard II*, *Richard III*, and *1 Henry IV*, all of which had originally been entered separately by Andrew Wise in 1597–8.[65] The copyright was transferred, *en bloc*, from him to Law on 25 June 1603,[66] the year Wise ceased bookselling and probably died. Law's zealous interest in the publication of playbooks never dwindled from 1601 to the end of his career. *Two Lamentable Tragedies*, published in 1601, was the earliest exemplar of a series of play-texts that he commissioned a trade printer to produce. In the following year, he hired Thomas Creede for the printing of the first quarto (hereafter Q1) of an anonymous comedy entitled as *How a Man May Choose a Good Wife from a Bad*.[67] The play was not entered, but Law somehow retained the right to reprint the subsequent editions. In 1604, Law started publishing one of Shakespeare's plays whose copyright he had obtained a year before, that is, Q4 *1 Henry IV*, with the text being printed by Valentine Simmes. In 1605, Law sold new copies of a reprint edition of two plays, namely, Q2 *How a Man May Choose* (by Simmes) and Q4 *Richard III* (by Creede). The three republished plays in two successive years probably helped his business, for in 1604–5, he sold only eight titles in all.[68] After a three-year break, Law published three quarto editions one after another in 1608; Q3 *How a Man May Choose* (1608, by John Windet), Q4 *Richard II*, as well as a variant of Q4 with new additions of a Parliament scene (1608, by William White), and Q5 *1 Henry IV* (1608, by Windet). Flourishing as it may seem, his business transactions evidently dwindled and he was helped by the three copyrighted plays, for they formed all the titles that he could sell in 1608. From 1612 to 1615, Law began reissuing a single play per year; he reprinted copies of Q5 *Richard III* (1612, by Creede), Q6 *1 Henry IV* (1613, by White), Q4 *How a Man May Choose* (1614, by White), and Q5 *Richard II* (1615, by

---

[65] See Arber, *Transcript*, iii. 89, 93, 105, respectively.   [66] Arber, *Transcript*, iii. 239.
[67] Greg, *Bibliography*, i. 303 (no. 191 (a)).
[68] It is uncertain why he avoided *Richard II* despite his acquisition of the copyright.

Thomas Purfoot). The eighteen titles he published in the four year period included these four reissued plays. Six years later, Law embarked yet again on republishing three plays, Q5 *How a Man May Choose* (1621, by Purfoot), Q6 *Richard III* (1622, by Purfoot), and Q7 *1 Henry IV* (1622, by Purfoot). His business in 1621–2 was shrinking drastically, for he produced only three titles in the two years. Q7 *Richard III* (1629, by John Norton) was republished in the year he retired, and this was the sole title that Law could sell in his final year. Between 1601 and 1629, Law published sixteen editions of only five plays, of which ten editions were of Shakespeare's history plays. The tactic of intermittent republishing of his copyrighted popular plays in 1604–5, 1608, 1612–15, and 1629 undoubtedly supported his unsteady business. The copy transfer of Shakespeare's plays from Wise to Law was clearly successful, for Law could rely on them whenever his bookshop's finances became weak. Law never republished *Two Lamentable Tragedies*. Presumably, he regarded its second edition as unattractive and unprofitable in view of competitive publishing business in London.

*

The play drew much attention to the question of its authorship in the nineteenth and the early twentieth centuries. Identification of the author formed the principal arena of debate, for nothing was known about a 'Rob. Yarington', and the play is the only known work written by him. One of the two plots, the so-called the Merry plot, was based on an actual murder by Thomas Merry of Robert Beach and his boy, Thomas Winchester, which occurred on 23 August 1594. Six days later, on 29 August, the titles for a pamphlet and a ballad on this event were entered in the Stationers' Registers; the former was entitled as '*A true discourse of a most cruell and barbarous murther committed by one THOMAS MERREY, on the persons of ROBERTE BEECHE and THOMAS WINCHESTER his servaunt. on ffridaie night the 23th. of August. beinge Bartholomue Eve. 1594. Together with the order of his array[g]nement and execucon.*', while the latter was a ballad called '*B[E]ECHE his ghoste. complayninge on ye wofull murder committed on him and THOMAS WINCHESTER his servaunt.*' After a short while, on 3, 7, and 9 September, four more ballads of various titles, which deal with the two culprits' executions, were entered one after another.[69] Of the six titles entered between 29 August and 9 September, five were entered by a team of stationers consisting of Thomas Gosson (bookseller), Thomas Millington (bookseller), and Thomas Dawson (printer), while the title entered on 3 September was by John Danter (printer).

---

[69] Arber, *Transcript*, ii. 658–59. Their titles were '*a lamentable ballad describing the wofull murder of ROBERT BEECHE &c*' (3 Sep.), '*the pitifull lamentacon of RACHELL MERRYE whoo suffred in Smithfeild with her brother THOMAS MERRYE the vjth of September 1594*', '*the lamentable ende of THOMAS MERRYE and RACHELL his Sister*' (7 Sep.), and '*lamentacon of THOMAS MERRYE &c*' (9 Sep.).

Clearly, the Gosson group formed a near-monopoly in publishing the highly topical material, but none of these stationers including Danter had kept their interest in producing the dramatic version of the event. The titles of the six lost items, consisting of a pamphlet and five ballads, are all we know of these works published shortly after the actual murder occurred in the summer of 1594.

Five years later, some curious payment records were inscribed by Philip Henslowe in his 'Diary'. In November and December 1599, Henslowe paid three dramatists for 'A tragedie called mereie [i.e. Merry]' and 'the tragedie of orphenes [i.e. Orphan's]'. The payment records of John Day, William Haughton, and Henry Chettle are as follows:[70]

Tragedy of Merry			*Orphan's Tragedy*		
1599					
21 November	Haughton	10 s			
27 November	Day & Haughton	20 s	27 November	Chettle	10 s
5 December	Day & Haughton	20 s			
6 December	Day	10 s			
6 December	Day & Haughton (full payment)	40 s			
1600					
10–18 January	Master of the Revels (licensing)	7 s	10 January (payment for *Italian Tragedy*)	Day	40 s
1601					
			24 September (part of payment)	Chettle	10 s

As early as in 1845, J. Paine Collier surmised that *The Tragedy of Merry* for which Day and Haughton received various sums 'may have been upon the same incidents as one of the plots' in *Two Lamentable Tragedies*, while *The Orphan's Tragedy* was possibly founded on the popular story of 'the Children in the Wood'.[71] In 1885, A. H. Bullen, editor of the play's earliest modern edition, stated in his Introduction that *Orphan's* for which Chettle received ten shillings has a title which 'at once reminds us of the second plot' of the play.[72] Frederick Gard Fleay carried these observations a step further in 1891 to conclude that Chettle consolidated Day and Haughton's *Merry* and his own *Orphan's* into a single play called *Two Lamentable Tragedies*; this was based on the fact that, on 24 September 1601, Chettle received 10 shillings again from

[70] *Henslowe's Diary*, 2nd edn, ed. R. A. Foakes (Cambridge, 2002), pp. 62, 127–8.
[71] *The Diary of Philip Henslowe, from 1591 to 1609: Printed from the Original Manuscript Preserved at Dulwich College*, ed. J. Paine Collier (London, 1845), pp. 92–3.
[72] Bullen, *A Collection*, iv. 1–3.

Henslowe. Fleay argued that the play as it stands was co-authored by Day, Haughton, and Chettle, and that 'Rob. Yarington' was 'a fictitious name.'[73]

At the start of the twentieth century, W. W. Greg provided a more detailed analysis of the authorship of the play, with his conjecture that Day, receiving forty shillings in earnest from Henslowe on 10 January 1600 for 'his Boock*e* called the etalyan tragedie' (which Fleay and Greg identified as *Orphan's* because of the second plot's setting, Padua) 'contributed a more or less independent underplot' to each tragedy, and that 'these were dropt when the main plots were amalgamated' by Chettle on 24 September 1601. Greg concluded that the play was the product of Haughton and Chettle, and that Yarington, a scribe, edited the entire play by inserting such curious stage directions as 'to the people' and by using some peculiar spellings throughout, and finally left his name at the end of the manuscript from which it somehow found its way on to the title-page.[74] One may well be inclined to believe this with the awareness that the playwright has a scrivener appear on stage in a scene (TLN 226–387) where he not only is assigned five speeches of his own (TLN 281, 297–9, 342–3, 348, 350) but reads a will (282–3).[75] Greg's argument was, however, doubtless unacceptable; Henslowe, after paying forty shillings to Day and Haughton as full payment on 6 December, obtained the performance licence of *Merry* by paying seven shillings to 'the m[r] of the Revelles man' between 10 and 18 January 1600. This means that *Merry* had been completed as a single play by the beginning of 1600 and had been waiting for performance; there is no reason for it to have been amalgamated with another play. And, in 1601, Chettle was evidently not paid for combining two plays as Greg suggested, but he merely received '*p*art of payment for A Boock*e* called th*e* orfenes [*Orphan's*] tragedy'[76]; one must do nothing more than read this note verbatim. The process in which *The Italian Tragedy* was completed obviously followed a different path from that of *Merry*, for Henslowe recorded a couple of payments to Wentworth Smith, another dramatist, for his 'etalleyon tragedie'; he received forty shillings in earnest on 7 March 1603, and four pounds as full payment on 12 March.[77] It took only five days, short compared with the normal four to six weeks,[78] to finish this play. This may perhaps indicate that Smith had received from Henslowe's archive Day's manuscript of *The Italian Tragedy*, prepared a little more than three years earlier but not finished, and revised it in a very short time.

Soon after Greg's argument was published, Robert Adger Law maintained in 1910 that the play was written by Yarington alone in 1594, and that the

[73] Frederick Gard Fleay, *A Biographical Chronicle of the English Drama 1559–1642*, 2 vols (London, 1891; repr. New York, [n.d.]), ii. 285–6.

[74] *Henslowe's Diary*, ed. W. W. Greg, 2 vols (London: 1904–8), II (Commentary), 208–9.

[75] A 'scrivener' is, however, not an extremely rare character. The play is one of twenty-two plays published in 1566–1641 in which a 'scrivener' appears. See Thomas L. Berger, William C. Bradford, and Sidney L. Sondergard, *An Index of Characters in Early Modern English Drama Printed Plays 1500–1660* (Cambridge, 1998), p. 88.

[76] Foakes, *Henslowe's Diary*, p. 182.   [77] Foakes, *Henslowe's Diary*, pp. 224–5.

[78] Neil Carson, *A Companion to Henslowe's Diary* (Cambridge, 1988), p. 59.

manuscript later fell into the hands of Henslowe. According to Law, Day and Haughton revised the Merry plot for *Merry*, while Chettle was in the process of revising the second plot for *Orphan's* but was unable to finish it. While the two tragedies no longer exist, Yarington's original finally was printed in 1601.[79] In 1917, Albert Croll Baugh discredited Greg's theory of Chettle amalgamating the two plays in 1601 by arguing that 'Bull' (TLN 1705), the hangman, had lived and performed his duty until 1597 but 'About this time [...] he must have died and have been succeeded by one Derrick'.[80] Subsequently, E. K. Chambers admitted in 1923 that there hardly is sufficient reason for denying Yarington the ascription on the title-page,[81] while S. R. Golding, in 1926, also sanctioned the single authorship of Yarington both in Merry's and Orphan's plots, based on the internal evidence that the play's peculiar spelling 'scripulous' (old form of 'scrupulous', TLN 409, 2076, 2332), parallel speeches, metre, and so on appear in both plots.[82]

In 1930, Bernard M. Wagner discovered the curious fact that 'Robt. Yarrington jun^r.' obtained freedom of the Scriveners' Company in 1603,[83] a clue to support Greg's old theory that Yarington was a scribe, not a playwright. Nevertheless, as there currently is no evidence that demonstrates a direct link of the scribe to the author of the play, it is reasonable to conclude, like many commentators, that the author of the play is none other than Yarington, the dramatist, whose name was clearly printed on the title-page as 'By ROB. YARINGTON.'[84] He probably wrote the text between late summer 1594 when the murder case actually occurred and *c.*1597 when the hangman Bull died or retired. Patenaude suggests that 'late 1594 to 1595 seems the most likely', for Yarington 'sought to capitalize on a market which had already supported the publication of five ballads and a "book" on the same events.'[85] The date she proposed sounds acceptable, because 'Truth' explains in the Induction that, of the two main plots, 'The one was done in famous London late' (TLN 95), and 'The most here present know this to be true' (102), while at the end of the play 'Truth' refers to the execution scene of Merry and Rachel that 'Which many heere did see performe'd indeed' (2402). Yarington would hardly have written such speeches long after the murder and execution had occurred. The records of payments to Day, Haughton, and Chettle in 1599 probably show Henslowe's attempt to recycle an old dramatic manuscript

[79] Law, 'Yarington's *Two Lamentable Tragedies*', pp. 167–77.
[80] 'William Haughton's *Englishmen for My Money*', ed. Albert Croll Baugh, doctoral thesis, University of Pennsylvania, 1917, p. 58. The name 'Bull' appears in *The Trimming of Thomas Nashe* published in 1597 (*STC* 12906, G4^r), sometimes attributed to Gabriel Harvey.
[81] E. K. Chambers, *The Elizabethan Stage*, 4 vols (Oxford, 1923), iii. 518.
[82] S. R. Golding, 'The Authorship of the *Two Lamentable Tragedies*', *Notes and Queries*, 151 (1926), 347–50.
[83] Bernard M. Wagner, 'Robert Yarrington', *Modern Language Notes*, 45 (1930), 147–8.
[84] Catherine Richardson, for example, is far from doubtful about Yarington's authorship and provides a thematic discussion in a chapter exclusively for that play, in her *Domestic Life and Domestic Tragedy in Early Modern England: The Material Life of the Household* (Manchester, 2006), pp. 128–49.
[85] Patenaude, 'Critical Old-Spelling Edition', p. 15.

from which to re-produce a number of new plays with the help of the three dramatists. In and around 1599, there seems to have existed a demand for crime drama and domestic tragedies, a fact suggested by the entrance and publication of *A Warning for Fair Women*, the publication of the second edition of *Arden of Faversham*, and Henslowe's multiple payments between 24 July and 14 October 1599 for 'the stepmothers tragedie' (four times) and 'the lamentable tragedie of pagge [page] of plemoth [Plymouth]' (three times).[86] *The Tragedy of Merry*, licensed in January 1600, must have been performed at the Rose probably during the early months of the year. Under these circumstances, the publication of Yarington's original play, in which the tragic story of Merry and Rachel and the scene of their execution were described in the form of drama, would have appeared a promising enterprise for Matthew Law. He probably procured the manuscript from Henslowe and hired Read for the printing of a few hundred copies of the quarto.

For Yarington's identity as 'putative playwright', Lena Cowen Orlin has provided a list of five candidates.[87] With the help of Orlin's *ODNB* article and with fresh evidence collected through my research, it has been possible to identify five contemporary Robert Yaringtons: [1] Robert Yarington (1572–) of St Mary Woolchurch Haw, son of Robert Yarington who married in 1564[88]; [2] Rob Yarranton, draper, freed on 2 August 1592[89]; [3] Robert Yarrington junior, scrivener, freed on 3 November 1603, son of Robert Yarrington, merchant taylor. On 19 June 1604, he witnessed as a professional scribe the will of a widow who lived in Surrey.[90] Mark Eccles discovered in 1991 that, in 1612, Antony Jeffes, a player of the Admiral's Men, paid bail for two men 'together with Robert "Yerrington", scrivener'[91]; [4] Robert Yerrington of St Nicholas Acons, merchant taylor[92]; and [5] Robart Yarrantonn of St Dionis Backchurch, whose will was signed on 18 January 1625.[93] Assuming that a

[86] *A Warning for Fair Women* (1599, *STC* 25089) was entered by William Aspley on 17 Nov. 1599, and printed by Valentine Simmes for Aspley; Q2 *Arden of Faversham* (1599, *STC* 734) was printed by James Roberts for Edward White; for Henslowe's payments, see Foakes, *Henslowe's Diary*, pp. 123–5.

[87] See her article in the online edition of *Oxford Dictionary of National Biography* (2004–13). <http://www.oxforddnb.com/view/article/30185, accessed 2 May 2013>.

[88] *The Transcript of the Registers of the United Parishes of S. Mary Woolnoth and S. Mary Woolchurch Haw, in the City of London, from Their Commencement 1538 to 1760*, ed. J. M. S. Brooke and A. W. C. Hallen (London, 1886), pp. 302, 342.

[89] Percival Boyd provides the year of freedom alone, in his edition of *Roll of the Drapers' Company of London* (Croydon, 1934), p. 207. For the exact date of freedom, I am indebted to Miss Penelope Fussell, Archivist of The Drapers' Company (private correspondence). I would like to thank her for checking the Wardens' accounts and the Freedom lists for me. Unfortunately, there remains nothing to suggest Yarranton's family details.

[90] *Surrey Wills*, compiled by the Surrey Record Society, vol. 4, no. 15 (London, 1920), p. 275.

[91] *Scriveners' Company Common Paper 1357–1628 with a Continuation to 1678*, ed. Francis W. Steer (London, 1968), p. 44; Mark Eccles, 'Elizabethan Actors II: E–J', *Notes and Queries*, 38 (1991), 454–61, esp. p. 460.

[92] *The Register Book of the Parish of St. Nicholas Acons, London 1539–1812*, ed. William Brigg (Leeds, 1890), p. 102.

[93] *Playhouse Wills 1558–1642: An Edition of Wills by Shakespeare and His Contemporaries in the London Theatre*, ed. E. A. J. Honigmann and Susan Brock (Manchester, 1993), pp. 145–6.

London apprentice had to be bound to his master for at least seven years before he was freed between the age of twenty-one to twenty-four at the earliest,[94] and that, in 1594–5, 'Yarington' would have been old enough to have access to, and compile information on, Thomas Merry's murder and the 'Children of the Wood' story for the sake of dramatization, Yarington [3] may have been too young to become a professional dramatist, for he was probably twelve to sixteen in 1594–5. In this respect, Yarington [2], draper and twenty-three to twenty-seven years old when the play was probably composed, may appear a more plausible candidate: it may be recalled that Law once was a book-publishing draper and published two books in 1595–6. Yarington [2] could have found easy access to Law within the drapers' company, if he had written the original manuscript. One could, however, never say anything definite about Yaringtons [1], [4], and [5], except that Yarington [4], merchant taylor, was possibly the father of Yarington [3]. Most recently, Andrew Gurr is still doubtful about Yarington's identity as a dramatist, and brings our attention to Yarington [3]: Gurr denies Yarington's authorship of the play, and regards him as 'the scribe of Haughton and Day's *Two Lamentable Tragedies* [...] his name at the end of the quarto suggests that Henslowe used him as a scribe'.[95] The unsettled question of the author's identity will, doubtless, continue.

[94] David Kathman, 'Grocers, Goldsmiths, and Drapers: Freemen and Apprentices in the Elizabethan England', *Shakespeare Quarterly*, 55 (2004), 1–49, esp. p. 4.
[95] Andrew Gurr, *Shakespeare's Opposites: The Admiral's Company 1594–1625* (Cambridge, 2009), pp. 101, 248 n, 288.

Two Lamentable Tragedies.

The one, of the murther of Maister Beech *a Chaundler in* Thames-streete, and his boye, done by *Thomas Merry*.

The other of a young childe mur- thered in a Wood by two Ruffins, *with the consent of his Vnckle.*

By ROB. YARINGTON.

LONDON
Printed for *Mathew Lawe*, and are to be solde at
his shop in Paules Church-yarde neere vnto
S. Austines gate, at the signe
of the Foxe. 1601.

Two Tragedies
in one.

Enter Homicide, *solus.*

THaue in vaine paſt through each ſtately
    ſtreete,
And blinde-fold turning of this happie
    towne,
For wealth , for peace , and goodlie
    gouernement,
Yet can I not finde out a minde, a heart
For blood and cauſeleſſe death to harbour in;
They all are bent with vertuous gainefull trade,
To get their needmentes for this mortall life,
And will not ſoile their well addicted harts:
With rape, extortion, murther, or the death,
Of friend or foe, to gaine an Empery.
I cannot glut my blood delighted eye;
With mangled bodies which do gaſpe and grone,
Readie to paſſe to faire *Elizium,*
Nor bath my greedie handes in reeking blood,
Of fathers by their children murthered:
When all men elſe do weepe, lament and waile,
The ſad exploites of fearefull tragedies,
It glads me ſo, that it delightes my heart,
To ad new tormentes to their bleeding ſmartes.
                Enter Auarice.
But here comes *Auarice,* as if he ſought,
Some buſie worke for his pernicious thought:

                                        Whe-

Whether so fast all griping *Auarice?*

Aua. Why what carst thou, I seeeke for one I misse.

Ho. I may supplie the man you wish to haue,

Aua. Thou seemes to be a bold audatious knaue,
I doe not like intruding companie,
That seeke to vndermine my secrecie.

Ho. Mistrust me not I am thy faithfull friend.

Aua. Many say so, that proue false in the end.

Ho. But turne about and thou wilt know my face,

  Aua. It may be so, and know thy want of grace,
What *Homicide* thou art the man I seeke:
I reconcile me thus vpon thy cheeke.   *Kisse, imbrace.*
Hadst thou nam'd blood and damn'd iniquitie,
I had for borne to bight so bitterlie.

  Hom. Knowst thou a hart wide open to receiue,
A plot of horred desolation,
Tell me of this, thou art my cheefest good,
And I will quaffe thy health in bowles of blood.

  Aua. I know two men, that seeme two innocents,
Whose lookes surueied with iuditiall eyes:
Would seeme to beare the markes of honestie,
But snakes finde harbour mongst the fairest flowers,
Then neuer credit outward semblaunces;

Enter Trueth.

I know their harts relentlesse mercilesse,
And will performe through hope of benefit:
More dreadfull things then can be thought vpon.

  Hom. If gaine will draw, I prethy then allure,
Their hungrie harts with hope of recompence,
But tye dispaire vnto those moouing hopes,
Vnleast a deed of murther farther it,
Then blood on blood, shall ouertake them all,
And we will make a bloodie feastiuall.

  Coue. The plots are laide, the keyes of golden coine,
Hath op'd the secret closets of their harts,
Inter, insult, make captiue at thy will,

Them-

Themselues, and friends, with deedes of damned ill:
Yonder is truth, she commeth to bewaile,
The times and parties that we worke vpon.
　Hom. Why let her weepe, lament, and morne for me,
We are right bred of damn'd iniquitie,
And will go make a two-folde Tragedie.　　*Exeunt.*
　Truth. Goe you disturbers of a quiet soule,
Sad, greedy, gaping, hungrie *Canibals,*
That ioy to practise others miseries;
Gentles, prepare your teare bedecked eyes,
To see two shewes of lamentation,
Besprinckled euery where with guiltlesse blood,
Of harmlesse youth, and pretie innocents,
Our Stage doth weare habilliments of woe,
Truth rues to tell the truth of these laments:
The one was done in famous London late,
Within that streete whose side the riuer Thames
Doth striue to wash from all impuritie:
But yet that siluer streame can neuer wash,
The sad remembrance of that cursed deede,
Perform'd by cruell *Merry* on iust *Beech,*
And his true boye poore *Thomas Winchester,*
The most here present, know this to be true:
Would truth were false, so this were but a tale,
The other further off, but yet too neere,
To those that felt and did the crueltie:
Neere *Padua* this wicked deed was done,
By a false Vncle, on his brothers sonne,
Left to his carefull education,
By dying Parents, with as strict a charge,
As euer yet death-breathing brother gaue:
Looke for no mirth, vnlesse you take delight,
In mangled bodies, and in gaping wounds,
Bloodily made by mercy wanting hands,
Truth will not faine, but yet doth grieue to showe,
This deed of ruthe and miserable woe.

A 3

Enter

Enter Merry.

I liue in meane and difcontented ftate,
But wherefore fhould I thinke of difcontent:
I am belou'd, I haue a pretty houfe,
A louing fifter, and a carefull man,
That doe not thinke their dayes worke well at end,
Except it bring me in fome benefit:
And well frequented is my little houfe,
With many gueftes and honeft paffengers,

Enter Beech *and a friend.*

Which may in time aduance my humble ftate,
To greater wealth and reputation.
And here comes friends to drinke fome beare or ale, *Sit in*
They are my neighbours, they fhall haue the beft, *his fhop.*
*Ne.*Come neighbor *Beech* lets haue our mornings draught
And wele go drinke it at yong *Merries* houfe:
They fay he hath the beft in all this towne,
Befides they fay he is an honeft man,
And keepes good rule and orders in his houfe.

Beech. He's fo indeede, his conuerfation,
Is full of honeft harmleffe curtefie:
I dare prefume, if that he be within,
Hele ferue vs well, and keepe vs company,
See where he is, go in, ile follow you.   *Striue curtefie;*
Nay ftraine no curtefie you fhall goe before.

Mer. Your welcome neighbour, you are welcome fir,
I praie fit downe, your verie welcome both:

Beech. We thanke you for it, and we thinke no leffe,
Now fill two cans of your ould ftrongeft beare:
That make fo manie loofe their little wits,
And make indentures as they go along.

Mer. Hoe fifter *Racheli:*   *Rach.*I come prefently.

Enter Rachell.

Mer. Goe draw thefe gentlemen two Cans of beare,
Your negligence that cannot tend the fhop,
Willl make our cuftomers forfake the houfe.
Wheres *Harry Williams* that he ftaies not here.

                    Rach.

Rach. My selfe was busie dressing vp the house,
As for your man he is not verie well:
But sitteth sleeping by the kitchen fier.

Mer. If you are busie get you vp againe,   *Exit.*
Ile draw my neighbours then their drinke my selfe,
Ile warrant you as good as any mans,
And yet no better, many haue the like.   *Exit for Beare.*

Neigh. This showes him for a plaine and honest man,
That will not flatter with too many wordes:
Some shriltong'd fellowes would haue cogd and faind,
Saying ile draw the best in Christendome.

Beech. Hees none of those, but beares an honest minde,
And shames to vtter what he cannot proue.

Enter Merry.

But here he comes, is that the best you haue,

Mer. It is the best vpon mine honest worde.

Beech. Then drinke to vs.   *Mer.* I drinke vnto you both.
Nei.Beech. We pledge you both, and thanke you hartelie.

Beech. Heres to you sir. *Neigh.* I thanke you,

          Maister Beech *drinkes, drinke* Neighbour.

Neigh. Tis good indeed and I had rather drinke,
Such beare as this as any Gascoine wine:
But tis our English manner to affect
Strange things, and price them at a greater rate,
Then home-bred things of better consequence.

Mer. Tis true indeede, if all were of your minde,
My poore estate would sooner be aduanc'd:
And our French Marchants seeke some other trade.

Beech. Your poore estate, nay neighbour say not so,
For God be thanked you are well to liue.

Mer. Not so good neighbour, but a poore young man,
That would liue better if I had the meanes:
But as I am, I can content my selfe,
Till God amend my poore abilitie.

Neigh. In time no doubt, why man you are but young,
And God assure your selfe hath wealth in store,
If you awaight his will with patience.
          A 4   *Beech.*

Beech. Thankes be to God I liue contentedlie,   190
And yet I cannot boast of mightie wealth:
But yet Gods blessings haue beene infinit,
And farre beyond my expectations,
My shop is stor'd, I am not much in debt;
And here I speake it where I may be bold,
I haue a score of poundes to helpe my neede,
If God should stretch his hand to visit me,
With sicknesse, or such like aduersity.

Neigh. Enough for this, now neighbour whats to pay,
Mer. Two pence good sir. *Beech.* Nay pray sir forbeare,   200
Ile pay this reckoning for it is but small.

Neigh. I will not striue since yee will haue it so.

Beech. Neighbour farewell.   *Exit Beech and neigh.*

Mer. Farewell vnto you both.
His shop is stor'd he is not much indebt,
He hath a score of poundes to helpe his neede,
I and a score too if the trueth were knowne:
I would I had a shop so stor'd with wares,
And fortie poundes to buy a bargaine with,
When as occasion should be offered me,   210
Ide liue as merrie as the wealthiest man,
That hath his being within London walles,
I cannot buy my beare, my bread, my meate:
My fagots, coales, and such like necessaries,
At the best hand, because I want the coine,
That manie misers coaser vp in bagges,
Hauing enough to serue their turnes besides:
Ah for a tricke to make this *Beeches* trash,
Forsake his cofer and to rest in mine,
I marrie sir, how may that tricke be done: 220
Marrie with ease and great facilitie,
I will inuent some new-found stratagem,
To bring his coyne to my possesshon;
What though his death relieue my pouertie,
Gaine waites on courage, losse on cowardice.

                                            Enter

8

Enter Pandino *and* Armenia *ficke on a bed,* Pertillo *their
foune,* Falleria *his brother,* Softrato *his wife,* Alinfo
their fonne, and a Scriuener *with a* VVill, *&c.*

Pan. Brother and fifter, pray you both drawe neere,
And heere my will, which you haue promifed
Shall be performde with wifhed prouidence,
This little Orphant I muft leaue behinde,
By your direction to be gouerned.
As for my wife and I, we do awaite,
The bleffed houre when it fhall pleafe the Lord,
To take vs to the iuft Ierufalem.
Our chiefeft care is for that tender boye,
Which we fhould leaue difcomfortleffe behinde,
But that we do affure vs of your loue,
And care to guide his weake vnhable youth,
In pathes of knowledge grace and godlineffe:
As for the riches of this mortall life,
We leaue enough, foure hundreth pounds a yeare,
Befides two thoufand pounds to make a ftocke,
In money, Iewels, Plate, and houfhold ftuffe,
Which yearely rents and goods we leaue to you,
To be furrendered into his hands,
When he attaines to yeeres of difcreation.
My Will imports thus much, which you fhall heare,
And you fhall be my fole Executor.

Fall. Brother and fifter how my hart laments,
To fee your weake and ficke afflicted limmes,
Neere ouercome with dyrefull malladies,
The God of heauen can truely teftifie,
Which to fpeake plaine, is nere a whit at all. *To the people,*
Which knowes the fecret corners of my heart,
But for the care you do impofe on me,
For the tuition of your little fonne,
Thinke my kinde brother, I will meditate,
Both day and night, how I may beft fulfill,

B   The

The care and trust, reposed in your Will,
And see him posted quickly after you.   *To the people.*
    Arm. Enough kinde brother, we assure vs so,
Else would we seeke another friend abroade,
To do our willes and dying Testament,
Nature and loue will haue a double care,
To bring him vp with carefull dilligence,
As best beseemes one of such parentage.
    Fall. Assure your selfe the safest course I can,
Shall be prouided for your little sonne,
He shall be sent vnto the King of heauen.   *To the people.*
    Sostr. Feare not good brother, and my louing sister,
But we will haue as tender care of him,
As if he were our owne ten thousand times:
God will be father of the fatherlesse,
And keepe him from all care and wretchednesse.
    Allenso. Vnekle and Aunt take comfort, I will see,
My little coozen haue no iniurie.
    Pan. Ar. We thanke you all, come let the Will be read.
    Fall. If it were seald, I would you both were dead.
    Scrine. Then giue attention, I will read the Will.
                Reade the VVill.
In the name of God, Amen. I, &c.
    Pan. Thus if my sonne miscarry, my deare brother,
You and your sonne shall then enioy the land,
And all the goods which he should haue possessd,
    Fall. If he miscarry, brother God forbid,
God blesse mine Nephew, that thine eyes may see,
Thy childrens children with prosperity:
I had rather see the little vrchin hangd,   *To the people.*
Then he should liue, and I forgoe the land.
    Ar. Thankes gentle brother, husband seale the Will.
    Pand. Giue me a Pen and Inke, first to subscribe,
I write so ill through very feeblenesse,
That I can scarcely know this hand for mine,
But that you all can witnesse that it is.
    Scri. Giue me the seale; I pray sir take it of,
                                This

270

280

290

This you deliuer for your latest Will,
And do confirme it for your Testament.

    Pand. With all my hart : here brother keepe my Will,
And I referre me to the will of God,
Praying him deale aswell with you and yours,
As you no doubt will deale with my poore child:
Come my *Pertillo,* let me blesse thee boy,
And lay my halfe dead hand vpon thy head,
God graunt those dayes that are cut off in me,
With ioy and peace may multiply in thee:
Be slowe to wrath, obey thy Vnckle still,
Submit thy selfe vnto Gods holy will,
In deede and word, see thou be euer true,
So brother, childe, and kinsfolkes all adue .   *He dyeth.*

    Per. Ah my deere mother, is my father dead ?

    Ar. I my sweete Boye, his soule to heauen is fled,
But I shall after him immediatly,
Then take my latest blessing ere I dye,
Come let me kisse thy little tender lips,
Cold death hath tane possession of thy mother.
Let me imbrace thee in my dying armes,
And pray the lord protect thee from al harmes:
Brother, I feare, this childe when I am gone,
Wil haue great cause of griefe & hideous feare:
You will protect him, but I prophecie,
His share will be of woe and misery:
But mothers feares do make these cares arise,
Come boye and close thy mothers dying eyes.
Brother and sister, here the latest words,
That your dead sister leaues for memory:
If you deale ill with this distressed boye,
God will reuenge poore orphants iniuries,
If you deale well, as I do hope you will,
God will defend both you and yours from ill.
Farewell, farewell, now let me breath my last,
Into his dearest mouth, that wanteth breath,
And as we lou'd in life imbrace in death;

                  B 2   Bro.

Brother and sister this is all I pray,
Tender my Boye when we are laide in clay.   *Dyeth.*

Allen. Gods holy Angell guide your louing soules,
Vnto a place of endlesse happinesse.

Softr. Amen, Amen, ah what a care she had,
Of her small Orphant, she did dying pray,
To loue her childe, when she was laide in claye.

Scr. Ah blame her not although she held it deare,
She left him yonge the greater cause of feare.

Fall. Knew she my minde it would recall her life, *To*
And like a staring Commet she would mooue, *the people.*
Our harts to thinke of desolation,
Scriuenor, haue you certified the will?

Scri. I haue.

Fall. Then theres two Duckets for your paines.

Scri. Thankes gentle sir, and for this time farewell. *Exit.*

Soft. Come prety coozen, cozened by grim death,
Of thy most carefull parents all too soone,
Weepe not sweete boy, thou shalt haue cause to say,
Thy Aunt was kinde, though parents lye in claye.

Pert. But giue me leaue first to lament the losse,
Of my deere Parents, nature bindeth me,
To waile the death of those that gaue me life,
And if I liue vntill I be a man,
I will erect a sumptuous monument,
And leaue remembrance to ensuing times,
Of kinde *Pandine* and *Armenia.*

Allen. That shall not neede, my father will erect,
That sad memoriall of their timeles death,
And at that tombe we will lament and say
Soft lye the bones of faire *Armenia.*

Fall. Surcease *Allenso*, thats a bootelesse cost,
The Will imports no such iniunction:
I will not spend my little Nephewes wealth,
In such vaine toyes, they shall haue funerall,
But with no stately ceremoniall pompe,
Thats good for nought but fooles to gase vppon;

                     Liue

340

350

360

370

Liue thou in hope to haue thine vnckles land.

   Allen. His land, why father you haue land enough,
And more by much then I do know to vſe:
I would his vertues would in me ſuruiue,
So ſhould my Vnckle ſeeme in me aliue,
But to your will I doe ſubmit my ſelfe,
Do what you pleaſe concerning funeralls.

   Fall. Come then away, that we may take in hand,
To haue poſſeſſion of my brothers land,
His goods and all vntill he come of age:
To rule and gouerne ſuch poſſeſſions,
That ſhalbe neuer or ile miſſe my marke,
Till I ſurrender vp my life to death:
And then my ſonne ſhalbe his fathers heire,
And mount aloft to honors happy chaire.

                         Exeunt: Omnes.

           Enter Merry ſolus.

Beech hath a ſcore of pounds to helpe his neede,
And I may ſtarue ere he will lend it me:
But in diſpight ile haue it ere I ſleepe,
Although I ſend him to eternall reſt,
But ſhallow foole, thou talkſt of mighty things,
And canſt not compaſſe what thou doſt conceiue:
Stay let me ſee, ile fetch him to my houſe,
And in my garret quickly murther him:
The night conceales all in her pitchie cloake,
And none can open what I meane to hide,
But then his boy will ſay I fetcht him foorth:
I am reſolu'd, he ſhall be murthered to,
This toole ſhall write, ſubſcribe, and ſeale their death,
And ſend them ſafely to another world:
But then my ſiſter, and my man at home,
Will not conceale it when the deede is done,
Tuſh one for loue, the other for reward,
Will neuer tell the world my cloſe intent,
My conſcience ſaith it is a damned deede:
To traine one foorth, and ſlay him priuily,

             B 3   Peace

Peace confcience, peace. thou art too fcripulous,
Gaine doth attended this refolution,
Hence daftard feare, I muft, I can, I will,
Kill my beft friend to get a bag of gold:
They fhall dye both, had they a thoufand liues,
And therefore I will place this hammer here,
And take it as I follow *Beech* vp ftaires,
That fuddenlie before he is aware,
I may with blowes dafh out his hatefull braines,
Hoe *Rachell*, bring my cloake, looke to the houfe,
I will returne againe immediatly.

  Rach. Here it is brother, I pray you ftay not long,
Guefle will come in, 'tis almoft fupper time.   *Ex. Ra.*

  Mer. Let others fuppe, ile make a bloudier feaft,
Then euer yet was dreft in *Merryes* houfe,
Be like thy felfe, then haue a merrie hart,
Thou fhalt haue gold to mend thy pouertie,
And after this, liue euer wealthilie.

      Then Merry *muft paffe to* Beeches *fhoppe, who*
        muft fit in his fhop, and Winchefter *his*
        boy ftand by: Beech *reading.*

What neighbour *Beech,* fo godly occupied?

  Beech. I maifter *Merry* it were better reade,
Then meditate on idle fantafies.

  Mer. You fpeake the trueth : there is a friend or two
Of yours, making merry in my houfe,
And would defire to haue your company.

  Beech. Know you their names?

  Mer. No truely nor the men.
I neuer ftoode to queftion them of that,
But they defire your prefence earneftlie.

  Beech. I pray you tell them that I cannot come,
Tis fupper time, and many will refort,
For ware at this time, aboue all other times;
Tis Friday night befides, and Bartholmew eue,
Therefore good neighbour make my iuft excufe.

  Mer. In trueth they told me that you fhould not ftay,
                         Goe

Goe but to drinke, you may come quick againe,
But not and if my hand and hammer hold.   *People.*

Beech. I am vnwilling, but I do not care,
And if I go to see the company.

Mer. Come quickly then, they thinke we stay too long,

Beech. Ile cut a peece of Cheese to drinke withall.

Mer. I take the farewell of your cutting knife,
Here is a hand shall helpe to cut your throate:
And giue my selfe a fairing from your chest :
What are you ready will you goe along ?

Beech. I now I am, boy looke you tend the shoppe,
If any aske, come for me to the Bull:
I wonder who they are that aske for me.

Mer. I know not that, you shall see presentlie,
Goe vp those staires, your friends do stay aboue,
Here is that friend shall shake you by the head,
And make you stagger ere he speake to you.

> *Then being in the vpper Rome* Merry *strickes
> him in the head fifteene times.*

Now you are safe, I would the boy were so,
But wherefore wish I, for he shall not liue,
For if he doe, I shall not liue my selfe.

> Merry *wiped his face from blood.*

Lets see what mony he hath in his purse,
Masse heres ten groates, heres something for my paine,
But I must be rewarded better yet.

> *Enter* Rachell *and* Harry Williams.

Wil. Who was it *Rachell* that went vp the staires?

Rach. It was my brother, and a little man
Of black complexion, but I know him not.

Wil. Why do you not then carry vp a light,
But suffer them to tarry in the darke.

Rach. I had forgot, but I will beare one vp.   *Exit vp.*

Wil. Do so I prethee, he will chide anon.   *Exit.*

> Rachell *speaketh to her brother.*

Rachell. Oh brother, brother, what haue you done?

Mer. Why murtherd one that would haue murtherd me.
                                                      Rach.

Rach. We are vndone, brother we are vndone,
What shall I say for we are quite vndone.
  Mer. Quiet thy selfe sister, all shalbe well,
But see in any case you do not tell,
This deede to *Williams* nor to any one:
  Rach. No, no, I will not, was't not maister *Beech*?
  Mer. It was, it is, and I will kill his man,   *Exit Rach.*
Or in attempting doe the best I can.

              Enter Williams *and* Rachell.
  Wil. What was the matter that you cride so lowde?
  Rach. I must not tell you, but we are vndone:
  VVill You must not tell me, but we are vndone,
Ile know the cause wherefore we are vndone.   *Exit vp.*
  Rach. Oh would the thing were but to doe againe,
The thought thereof doth rent my hart in twaine,
              Williams *to* Merry *aboue.*   *She goes vp.*
  Wil. Oh maister, maister, what haue you done?
  Mer. Why slaine a knaue that would haue murtherd
Better to kill, then to be kild my selfe.   (me.
  Wil. With what? wherewith? how haue you slaine the mã?
  Mer. Why with this hammer I knockt out his braines.
  VVil. Oh it was beastly so to butcher him,
If any quarrell were twixt him and you:
You should haue bad him meete you in the field,
Not like a coward vnder your owne roofe;
To knock him downe as he had bin an oxe,
Or silly sheepe prepard for slaughter house:
The Lord is iust, and will reuenge his blood,
On you and yours for this extremitie.
I will not stay an hower within your house,
It is the wickedst deed that ere was done.
  Mer. Oh sir content your selfe, all shall be well,
Whats done already, cannot be vndone.
  Rach. Oh would to God, the deed were now to do,
And I were priuie to your ill intent,
You should not do it then for all the world.
But prethie *Harry* do not leaue the house,

                                          For

For then fufpition will arife thereof,
And if the thing be knowne we are vndone.

VVil. Forfake the houfe, I will not ftay all night,
Though you will giue the wealth of Chriftendome.

Mer. But yet conceale it, for the loue of God,
If otherwife, I know not what to do.

VVil. Here is my hand, ile neuer vtter it,
Affure your felfe of that, and fo farewell.

Mer. But fweare to me, as God fhall helpe thy foule,
Thou wilt not tell it vnto any one.

VVil. I will not fweare, but take my honeft worde,
And fo farewell, my foule affureth me,   *Exit Merry*
God will reuenge this damn'd iniquitie.   *and Rach.*
What fhall become of me vnhappie wretch?
I dare not lodge within my Maifters houfe,
For feare his murthrous hand fhould kill me too,
I will go walke and wander vp and downe,
And feeke fome reft, vntill the day appeare:
At the Three-Cranes, in fome Haye loft Ile lye,
And waile my Maifters comming miferie.   *Exit.*

Enter Fallerio *folus.*

Fall. I haue poffeffion of my brothers goods,
His tennants pay me rent, acknowledge me
To be their Landlord, they frequent my houfe,
With Turkeys, Capons, Pigeons, Pigges and Geefe,
And all to gaine my fauour and good will.
His plate, his Iewels, hangings, houfhould ftuffe,
May well befeeme to fit a demie King,
His ftately buildings, his delightfull walkes,
His fertile Meadowes, and rich ploughed lands,
His well growne woods and ftor'd Fifhing ponds,
Brings endleffe wealth, befides continuall helpe,
To keepe a good and hofpitable houfe :
And fhall I ioy thefe pleafures but a time,
Nay brother, fifter, all fhall pardon me,
Before Ile fell my felfe to penurie.

         C   The

The world doth know,thy brother but resign'd,
The lands and goods,vntill his sonne attain'de,
To riper yeares to weld and gouerne them,
Then openly thou canst not do him wrong,
He liuing : there's the burthen of the song. 560
Call it a burthen,for it seemes so great
And heauie burthen,that the boy should liue,
And thrust me from this height of happinesse:
That I will not indure so heauie waight,
But shake it off,and liue at libertie,
Free from the yoake of such subiection,
The boy shall dye,were he my fathers sonne,
Before Ile part with my possession.
Ile call my sonne, and aske his good aduice,
How I may best dispatch this serious cause: 570
Hoe sir *Allenso*? *Alle.* Father. *Fall.* Hearken sonne,
I must intreate your furtherance and aduise,
About a thing that doth concerne vs neere,
First tell me how thou doost affect in heart,
Little *Pertillo*, thy dead Vnckles sonne.

  Allen. So well good father,that I cannot tell,
Whether I loue him dearer then my selfe :
And yet if that my heart were calde to count,
I thinke it would surrender me to death,
Ere young *Pertillo* should sustaine a wrong. 580

  Fall. How got his safetie such a deepe regarde
Within your heart,that you affect it so?

  Allen. Nature gaue roote,loue,and the dying charge,
Of his dead father,giues such store of sap,
Vnto this tree of my affection,
That it will neuer wither till I dye.

  Fall. But nature,loue,and reason,tels thee thus,
Thy selfe must yet be neerest to thy selfe.

  Allen. His loue dooth not estrange me from my selfe,
But doth confirme my strength with multitudes, 590
Of benefits,his loue will yeelde to me.

  Fall. Beware to foster such pernicious snakes,

                         With-

Within thy bosome, which will poyson thee.

Allen He is a Doue, a childe, an innocent,
And cannot poyson, father though he would.

Fall. I will be plainer, know *Pertillos* life,
Which thou doost call, a Doue, an innocent:
A harmlesse childe, and, and I know not what,
Will harme thee more, then any Serpent can,
I, then the very sight of Basiliskes.

Allen. Father, you tell me of a strange discourse,
How can his life produce such detriment,
As Basiliskes, whose onely sight is death?

Fall. Harken to me, and I will tell thee how:
Thou knowst his fathers goods, his houses, lands,
Haue much aduaunc'd our reputation,
In hauing but their vsage for a time,
If the boy liue, then like to sencelesse beasts,
Like longd eard Asses, and riche laden Mules,
We must resigne these treasures to a boye,
And we like Asses feede on simple Haye:
Make him away, they shall continue ours,
By vertue of his fathers Testament,
The Iewels, castles, medowes, houses, lands,
Which thy small cozen, should defeate thee of,
Be still thine owne, and thou aduance thy selfe,
Aboue the height of all thine Auncestours.

Allen. But if I mount by murther and deceite,
Iustice will thrust aspiring thoughts belowe,
And make me caper for to breake my neck:
After some wofull lamentation,
Of my obedience to vnlawfulnesse:
I tell you plaine, I would not haue him dye,
Might I enioy the *Soldans* Emperie.

Fall. What wilt thou barre thy selfe of happinesse,
Stop the large streame of pleasures which would flowe,
And still attend on thee like Seruingmen:
Preferre the life of him that loues thee not,
Before thine owne, and my felicitie.

C 2

Allen.

Allen. Ide rather choofe to feede on carefulneffe, 630
To ditche, to delue, and labour for my bread,
Nay rather choofe to begge from doore to doore,
Then condifcend to offer violence,
To young *Pertillo* in his innocence,
I know you fpeake, to found what mightie fhare,
Pertillo hath in my affection.

    Fall. In faith I do not, therefore prethie fay,
Wilt thou confent to haue him made away.

    Allen. Why then in faith, I am afhamde to thinke, 640
I had my being from fo foule a lumpe
Of adulation and vnthankfulneffe,
Ah, had their dying praiers no auaile
Within your hart ? no, damnd extorcion,
Hath left no roome for grace to harbor in,
Audacious finne, how canft thou make him fay,
Confent to make my brothers fonne away.

    Fall. Nay if you ginne to brawle, withdraw your felfe,
But vtter not the motion that I made,
As you loue me, or do regarde your life.

    Allen. And as you loue my fafetie, and your foule, 650
Let grace, and feare of God, fuch thoughts controule.

    Fall. Still pratling, let your grace and feare alone,
And leaue me quickly to my priuate thoughts,
Or, with my fworde Ile open wide a gate,
For wrath and bloudie death to enter in.

    Allen. Better you gaue me death and buriall,
Then fuch foule deeds fhould ouerthrow vs all.

    Fall. Still are you wagging that rebellious tounge,
Ile dig it out for Crowes to feede vpon,
If thou continue longer in my fight.   *Exit Allenfo.* 660
He loues him better then he loues his life,
Heres repetition of my brothers care,
Of fifters chardge, of grace, and feare of God,
Feare daftards, cowards, faint hart run-awayes,
Ile feare no coulours to obteine my will,
Though all the fiends in hell were oppofite,

                      Ide

Ide rather loofe mine eye, my hand, my foote,
Be blinde, wante fences, and be euer lame,
Then be tormented with fuch difcontent,
This refignation would afflict me with,
Be blithe my boy, thy life fhall fure be done,
Before the fetting of the morrowe funne.

Enter Auarice *and* Homicide *bloody.*
Hom. Make haft, runne headlong to deftruction,
I like thy temper, that canft change a heart,
From yeelding flefh, to Flinte and Adamant,
Thou hitft it home, where thou dooft faften holde,
Nothing can feperate the loue of golde.
Aua. Feare no relenting, I dare pawne my foule,
(And thats no gadge, it is the diuels due)
He fhall imbrew his greedie griping hands,
In the dead bofome of the bloodie boy,
And winde himfelfe, his fonne, and harmleffe wife,
In endleffe foldes of fure deftruction.
Now *Homicide,* thy lookes are like thy felfe,
For blood, and death, are thy companions,
Let my confounding plots but goe before,
And thou fhalt wade vp to the chin in gore.
Homi. I finde it true, for where thou art let in,
There is no fcrupule made of any finne,
The world may fee thou art the roote of ill,
For but for thee, poore *Beech* had liued ftill.   *Exeunt.*

Enter Rachel *and* Merry.
Rach. Oh my deare brother, what a heape of woe,
Your rafhneffe hath powrd downe vpon your head:
Where fhall we hide this trumpet of your fhame,
This timeleffe ougly map of crueltie?
Brother, if *VVilliams* do reueale the truth,
Then brother, then, begins our fceane of ruthe.
Mer. I feare not *VVilliams* but I feare the boy,
Who knew I fetcht his maifter to my houfe.
Rach. What doth the boy know wherabouts you dwel?
C 3   *Mer.*

Mer. I that tormentes me worse then panges of hell,
He must be slaine to, else hele vtter all.

   Rach. Harke brother, harke, me thinkes I here on call.

   Mer. Go downe and see, pray God my man keep close:
If he proue long-tongd then my daies are done,
The boy must die, there is no helpe at all:
For on his life, my verie life dependes,
Besides I cannot compasse what I would,
Vnlesse the boy be quicklie made away,
This that abridgde his haplesse maisters daies,
Shall leaue such sound memorials one his head,
That he shall quite forget who did him harme,
Or train'd his maister to this bloodie feast:
Why how now *Rachell*? who did call below?

         Enter Rachell.

   Rach. A maide that came to haue a pennie loafe.

   Mer. I would a pennie loafe cost me a pound,
Prouided *Beeches* boy had eate his last.

   Rach. Perchaunce the boy doth not remember you.

   Mer. It maie be so, but ile remember him.   *to people.*
And send him quicklie with a bloodie scrowle,
To greete his maister in another world.

   Rach. Ile goe to *Beeches* on a faind excuse,
To see if he will aske me for his maister.

   Mer. No, get you vp, you shall not stir abroade,
And when I call, come quicklie to the dore.

   Rach. Brother, or that, or any thing beside,
To please your minde, or ease your miserie.   *Exit.*

   Mer. I am knee deepe, ile wade vp to the wast,
To end my hart of feare, and to attaine,
The hoped end of my intention?
But I maie see, if I haue eyes to see,
And if my vnderstanding be not blind,
How manie dangers do alreadie waight,
Vpon my steppes of bold securitie,
Williams is fled, perchaunce to vtter all,
Thats but perchance, naie rather flatlie no,

                       But

But should he tell,I can but die a death,
Should he conceale,the boy would vtter it,
The boy must die,there is no remedie.

The boy sitting at his maisters dore.

VVin. I wonder that my maister staies so long,
He had not wont to be abroade so late:
Yonder comes one,I thinke that same is he.

Mer. I see the boye sits at his maisters doore,
Or now, or neuer, *Merry* stir thy selfe,
And rid thy hart from feare and iealousie:
Thomas Winchester go quicklie to your shoppe,
What sit you still,your maister is at hand.

When the boy goeth into the shoppe Merrie *striketh
fiue blowes on his head & with the seauenth leaues
the hammer sticking in his head, the boy groaning
must be heard by a maide who must crye to her
maister.* Merrie *flieth.*

Mai. Oh God I thinke theres theeues in *Beeches* shop.

*Enter one in his shirt and a maide,and comming to
Beeches shop findes the boy murthered.*

Nei. What cruell hand hath done so foule a deede,
Thus to bemangle a distressed youth:
Without all pittie or a due remorse,
See how the hammer sticketh in his head,
Wherewith this honest youth is done to death,
Speake honest *Thomas*,if any speach remaine,
What cruell hand hath done this villanie:
He cannot speake,his sences are bereft,
Hoe neighbour *Loney*, pray come downe with speede,
Your tennant *Beeches* man is murthered.

Loney sleeping. What would you haue some Mustard?

Nei. Your tennant *Beeches* man, is murthered.

Lo. Whose smothered,I thinke you lack your wit, *Out
What neighbor? what make you here so late?* *at a window.*

Nei. I was affrighted by a sodaine crie,
And comming downe found maister *Beeches* man,
Thus with a hammer sticking in his head. *Comes downe.*

C 4   *Loney.*

Lovey. Ah wo is me for *Thomas Winchester,*
The truest soule that euer maister had,
Wheres maister *Beech? Neigh.* Nay, no body can tell:
Did you see any running from the dore,   780
When you lookt out and heard the youngman crie,

   Maid. Yes I saw two trulie to my thinking, but they
Ranne away as fast as their hands could beare them:
By my troth twas so darke I could see no bodie, *To people.*
Pray God maister *Beech* hath not hurt his boy in his pati-
And if he haue he must be hangd in his choller.   (ence

   Lo. I dare be sworne he would not strike him thus,
Praie God his maister be not slaine himselfe.
The night growes late, and we will haue this course
Be watch'd all night, to morrow we shall see,   790
Whence sprang this strange vnciuill crueltie.

   Nei. Neighbour good night. *Lon.* Neighbors all good
   Ma. Praie God I neuer see so sad a sight.   (night.
                               Exeunt omnes.

       Enter Merry *knocking at the doore, and* Rachell
                 comes downe.

   Mer. Oh sister, sister, now I am pursu'd,
The mightie clamour that the boy did make,
Hath raisde the neighbours round about the street: 800
So that I know not where to hide my selfe.

   Ra. What brother, haue you kild *Beeches* boy?

   Mer. No, no, not I, but yet another hath,
Come, come to bed, for feare we be discri'd:
The fearefullest night that euer *Merry* knew.   *Exeunt.*
        Enter Falleria *and two Ruffaines.*

   Fal. Seeme it not strange resolued gentleman,
That I thus priuatelie haue seuered you,
To open secret sorrowes of my hart:
Thinke not I do intend to vndermine,   810
Your passed liues, although you know I am,
A man to whom the true vnpartiall sworde,
Of equall iustice is deliuered,
Therefore sweare both, as you respect your soules,

                                   At

At the laſt dreadfull ſeſſions held in heauen,
Firſt to conceale, and next to execute,
What I reueale, and ſhall enioyne you to.

    Both. So you rewarde vs, whatſoeuer it be,
We vowe performance, and true ſecreſie.

    Fall. There go aſide, yee ſeeming ſemblances,
Of equall iuſtice, and true pietie,
And lay my hearts corrupted Cytadell,
Wide open to your thoughts to looke into.
Know I am nam'd *Fallerio*, to deceiue
The world with ſhew of truth and honeſtie,
But yet nor truth, nor honeſtie abides,
Within my thoughts, but falſhood, crueltie,
Blood ſucking *Auarice*, and all the ſinnes,
That hale men on to bloodie ſtratagems,
Like to your ſelues, which care not how you gaine,
By blood, extorcion, falſhood, periurie,
So you may haue a pleaſing recompence: *They ſtart.*
Start not aſide, depart not from your ſelues,
I know your compoſition is as mine,
Of bloud, extortion, falſhood, periurie,
True branded with the marke of wickedneſſe.

    1. Ruffin. Be not ſo bitter, we are they indeede,
That would depriue our fathers of their liues,
So we were ſure to haue a benefit:
I way no more the murthring of a child,
Drag'd from the ſucking boſome of his mother,
Then I reſpect to quaffe a boule of wine,
Vnto his health, that dearely loueth me.

    2 Ruff. Where golde rewardeth, were apparent death
Before mine eyes, bolde, hartie, viſible,
Ide wraſtle with him for a deadly fall,
Or I would looſe my guerdon promiſed:
Ide hang my brother for to weare his coate,
That all that ſawe me might haue cauſe to ſay,
There is a hart more firme then Adamant,
To practiſe execrable butcheries.

D

Fall.

Fall. I know that well, for were I not assur'd,
Of your performance in this enterprice,
I would not ope the closet of my brest,
To let you know my close intention,
There is a little boy, an vrchin lad,
That stands betweene me and the glorious rayes,
Of my soule-wishing sunne of happinesse:
There is a thicket ten miles from this place,
Whose secret ambush, and vnvsed wayes,
Doth seeme to ioyne with our conspiracie,
There murther him, and when the deed is done,
Cast his dead body in some durtie ditch,
And leaue him for the Fowles to feed vpon:
Do this, here is two hundreth markes in golde,
To harten on your resolution:
Two hundreth more, after the deed is done,
Ile pay you more for satisfaction.

1. Ruff. Swones her's rewards would make one kill him-
To leaue his progenie so rich a prize,   (selfe,
Were twentie liues engadged for this coine,
Ide end them all, to haue the money mine.

2. Ruff. Who would not hazard life, nay soule and all,
For such a franke and bounteous pay-maister,
Sblood, what labour is't to kill a boy,
It is but thus, and then the taske is done,
It grieues me most, that when this taske is past,
I haue no more to occupie my selfe,
Two hundreth markes to giue a paltrie stab,
I am impacient till I see the brat.

Fall. That must be done with cunning secrecie,
I haue deuisde to send the boye abroade,
With this excuse, to haue him fostred,
In better manners then this place affoords,
My wife, though loath indeed to part with him,
Yet for his good, she will forgoe her ioy,
With hope in time to haue more firme delights,
Which she expects from young *Pertillos* life.

2. *Ruff.*

2.Ruff. Call you him *Pertillo,* faith leaue out the *T.*
Fall. Why so?   *Ruff.* Because *Perillo* will remaine,
For he shall surely perish if I liue :
What do you call the father of the child?

Fall. Why man, he hath no father left aliue.

1.Ruff. Yes such a father, that doth see and know,
How we do plot this little infants woe.   *To the people.*

2.Ruff. Why then his little sonne is much to blame,
That doth not keepe his father company.
When shall we haue deliuerie of the boy?

Fall. To morrow morning by the breake of day,
And you must sweare youle see him safely brought,
Vnto the place that I do send him to.

2.Ruff. That may we safely, for you meane to send
Him to the wood, and there his iourney ends:
Both soule and limbes shall haue a place to rest,
In earth the last, the first in *Abrams* brest.

Fall. Come gentlemen, this night go rest with me,
To morrow end *Pertillos* tragedie.   *Exeunt omnes.*

Enter Merry *and* Rachell.

Mer. Sister, now all my golde expected hopes,
Of future good, is plainely vanished,
And in her stead, grim visadged dispaire,
Hath tane possession of my guiltie heart,
Desire to gaine, began this desperate acte,
Now plaine apparance of destruction,
Of soule and body, waights vpon my sinne,
Although we hide our sinnes from mortall men,
Whose glasse of knowledge is the face of man,
The eye of heauen beholdes our wickednesse,
And will no doubt reuenge the innocent.

Rach. Ah, do not so disconsolate your selfe,
Nor adde new streames of sorrow to your griefe,
Which like a spring tide ouer-swels the bankes,
Least you do make an inundation,
And so be borne away with swiftest tides,

D 2   *Of*

Of vgly feare, and strong difpairing thoughts,
I am your fifter, though a filly Maide,
Ile be your true and faithfull comforter.

 Mer. *Rachel*, I fee thy loue is infinite,
And forrow had fo borne my thoughts away,
That I had almoft quite forgot my felfe,
Helpe me deare fifter to conuey from hence,   930
The fpectacle of inhumanitie.

 Rach. Whether would you conuey this lumpe of duft,
Vntimely murthred by your luckleffe hand.

 Mer. To the lowe roome, where we will couer it,
With Fagots, tell the euening doe approche:
In the meane time I will bethinke my felfe,
How I may beft conuey it foorth of doores,
For if we keepe it longer in the houfe,
The fauour will be felt throughout the ftreete,   940
Which will betray vs to deftruction.
Oh what a horror brings this beaftlineffe,
This chiefe of finnes, this felfe accufing crime
Of murther: now I fhame to know my felfe,
That am eftrang'd fo much from that I was,
True, harmleffe, honeft, full of curtefie,
Now falfe, deceitfull, full of iniurie:
Hould thou his heeles, ile beare his wounded head,
Would he did liue, fo I my felfe were dead.

    Bring downe the body, and couer it ouer with
      Faggots, himfelfe.   950

 Rach. Thofe little ftickes, do hide the murthred courfe,
But ftickes, nor ought befides, can hide the finne:
He fits on high, whofe quick all feeing eye,
Cannot be blinded by mans fubtilties.

 Mer. Looke euery where, can you difcerne him now?
 Rach. Not with mine eye, but with my heart I can.
 Mer. That is becaufe thou knoweft I laide him there,
To guiltineffe each thought begetteth feare:
But go my true, though wofull comforter,
Wipe vp the blood in euery place aboue,   960

                  So

So that no drop be found about the house,
I know all houses will be searcht anon:
Then burne the clothes, with which you wipe the ground
That no apparant signe of blood be found.

   Rach. I will, I will, oh would to God I could,
As cleerely wash your conscience from the deed,
As I can cleanse the house from least suspect,
Of murthrous deed, and beastly crueltie.

   Mer. Cease to wish vainely, let vs seeke to saue,
Our names, our fames, our liues, and all we haue. *Exeunt.*

    Enter three or foure neighbours together

   1. Neigh. Neighbours, tis bruted all about the towne,
That *Robert Beech* a honest Chaundelor,
Had his man deadly wounded yester night,
At twelue a clock, when all men were a sleepe.

   2. Where was his maister, when the deed was done.

   3. No man can tell, for he is missing to,
Some men suspect that he hath done the fact,
And that for feare the man is fled away,
Others, that knew his honest harmlesse life,
Feare that himselfe is likewise made away.

   4. Then let commaundement euery where be giuen,
That sinkes and gutters, priuies, creuises,
And euery place, where blood may be conceald,
Be throughly searcht, swept, washt, and neerely sought,
To see if we can finde the murther out:
And least that *Beech* be throwne into the *Thames,*
Let charge be giuen vnto the Watermen,
That if they see the body of a man,
Floting in any place about the *Thames,*
That straight they bring it vnto *Lambert hill,*
Where *Beech* did dwell when he did liue in health.

   1. Neigh. Ile see this charge performd immediatly.

   4. Now let vs go to Maister *Beeches* shop,   *Exit.*
To see if that the boy can giue vs light,
Of those suspitions which this cause doth yeeld.

D 3   2. This

2. This is the house call maister *Loney* forth,

3. Hoe maister *Loney*, doth the boy yet liue, *Ent. Loney*
Or can he vtter who hath done him wrong.

Lo. He is not dead but hath a dying life,
For neither speech, nor any sence at all,
Abideth in the poore vnhappie youth.

4. Here you of anie where his maister is.

Lo. No would we could, we all that knew his life,
Suspect him not for any such offence.

4. Bring forth the boy, that we may see his wounds.

> *Bringes him forth in a chaire, with a hammer*
> *sticking in his head.*

What say the Surgions to the yongmans woundes,

Lo. They giue him ouer, saying euerie wound
Of sixe, whereof ther's seauen in his head,
Are mortall woundes and all incurable.

> *They suruey his woundes.*

Enter Merrie, *and* Williams.

Mer. How now good *Harry*, hast thou hid my fault?
The boy that knew I train'd his maister forth:
Lies speechlesse, and euen at the point of death,
If you proue true, I hope to scape the brunt,

VVil. Whie feare not me, I haue conceal'd it yet,
And will conceale it, haue no doubt of me.

Mer. Thankes gentle *Harry*, thou shalt neuer lacke,
But thou and I will liue as faithfull friendes,
And what I haue, shalbe thine owne to vse:
There is some monie for to spend to day,
I know you meane to goe and see the faire.

Wil. I faine would go, but that I want a cloake.

Mer. Thou shalt not want a cloake, or ought beside,
So thou wilt promise to be secret: *Giue him his cloake.*
Here take my cloake, ile weare my best my selfe,
But where did you lie this last night?

Wil. At the three Cranes, in a Carmans hay-loft,
But ile haue better lodging soone at night,

Mer.

Mer. Thou wilt be secret, I will go and fee, *Exit Willi.*
What ftir they keepe about *Beeches* fhop,
Becaufe I would auoyde fufpition.   *Go to them.*
God faue you gentlemen, is this the boy
That is reported to be murthered?

4. He is not dead outright, but pleaf'd it God,
Twere better he had left this wicked world,
Then to liue thus in this extremitie.

Mer. A cruell hand no doubt that did the deede,
Whie pull you not the hammer from his head.

4. That muft not be before the youth be dead,
Becaufe the crowner and his queft may fee,
The manner how he did receiue his death:
Beare hence the bodie, and endeuor all,
To finde them out that did the villanie.

              Exeunt omnes : manet Merrie.

Mer. Do what you can, caft all your wits about,
Rake kennells, gutters, feeke in euerie place,
Yet I will ouergoe your cunning heads,
If *VVilliams* and my fifter hold their tongues :
My neighbours holdes not me in leaft fufpect,
Weighing of my former conuerfation :
Were *Beeches* boy well conueid awaie,
Ide hope to ouerblow this ftormie day.   *Exit.*

        Enter Falleria, Softrata, Allenfo, Pertillo : *and*
                  two Murtherers booted.

Fall. Now little cooze, you are content to goe
From me your vnckle and your louing Aunt,
Your faithfull cozen and your deareft friendes:
And all to come to be a skilfull man,
In learned artes and happie fciences.

Per. I am content, becaufe it pleafeth you,
My father bid I fhould obey your will,
And yeelde my felfe to your difcretion;
Befides my cozen gaue me yefternight,
A prettie Nag to ride to *Padua,*

          D 4   Of

Of all my friends *Alenſo* loues me beſt.

    Fall. I thinke thou art inſpir'd with propheſie,   *To the*
He loues thee better then I would he did: *people.*
Why wherefore thinke you ſo my pretie Nephew?

    Per. Becauſe he taught me how to ſay my prayers,
To ride a horſe, to ſtart the fearefull Hare,
He gaue this dagger to me yeſter night,
This little Ring, and many pretie things:
For which, kinde cooze, I reſt your true debtor,
And one day I will make you recompence.

    Fall. I, with thy lands and goods thou leau'ſt behinde.

    Alen. Pray father let me go along with him:
Now by the ſauiour of my ſinfull ſoule,   *To the people.*
I do not like thoſe fellowes countenance.

    Fall. Sonne be content, weele go a ſeauenight hence,
And ſee him in his vniuerſitie weedes :
Theſe will conduct him ſafely to the place,
Be well aſſured they'l haue a care of him,
That you ſhall neuer ſee *Pertillo* more.   *To the people.*

    Allen. Father, I pray you to withdraw your ſelfe,
Ide haue a word or two in ſecreſie.   *They ſpeake together.*

    Soſt. Come liuing image of thy dead mother,
And take my louing farewell, ere we part,
I loue thee dearly for thy fathers ſake,
But for thy mothers, doate with iealouſie,
Oh I do feare, before I ſee thy face,
Or thou, or I, ſhall taſte of bitterneſſe :
Kiſſe me ſweete boy, and kiſſing folde thine Aunte,
Within the circle of thy little armes,
I neede not feare, death cannot offer wrong,
The maieſtie of thy preſaging face,
Would vanquiſh him though nere ſo terrible,
The angrie Lioneſſe that is bereau'd,
Of her imperious crew of forreſt kings,
Would leaue her furie and defend thee ſafe,
From Wolues, from Panthers, Leopards, and ſhee Beares,
That liue by rapine, ſtealth, and crueltie,

                                        There-

1070

1080

1090

1100

Therefore to God I do commend thy ſtate,
Who will be ſure to guarde thee tenderly.
And now to you,that carry hence this wealth,
This precious iewell,this vnprized good,
Haue a regarde to vſe him carefully,
When he is parted from that ſerious care,
Which was imployde for his ſecuritie:
I vrge it not,that I miſdoubt your truth,
I hope his Vnckle doth perſwade himſelfe,
You will be courteous,kinde and affable,
Ther's ſome rewarde for hoped carefulneſſe.

Allen. Now by my ſoule I do ſuſpect the men,
Eſpecially the lower of the two:
See what a hollow diſcontented looke
He caſts,which brings apparant cauſe of feare,
The other,though he ſeeme more courteous,
Yet dooth his lookes preſadge this thought in me,
As if he ſcorn'd to thinke on courteſie.

Fall. Vpon my life,my ſonne you are to blame,
The gentlemen are honeſt,vertuous,
And will protect *Pertillo* happily:
Theſe thoughts proceed out of aboundant loue,
Becauſe you grieue to leaue his company:
If ought betide him otherwiſe then well,
Let God require due vengaunce on my head,
And cut my hopes from all proſperitie.

Allen. A heauie ſentence,full of wondrous feare,
I cannot chooſe but credit ſuch a vowe,
Come hether then, my ioy,my chiefeſt hopes.
My ſecond ſelfe,my earthly happineſſe,
Lend me thy little prety cherry lip,
To kiſſe me cozen, lay thy little hand
Vpon my cheeke,and hug me tenderly,
Would the cleere rayes of thy two glorious ſunnes,
Could penetrate the corners of my heart,
That thou might ſee,how much I tender thee.
My friends beholde within this little bulke,

E

Two

33

Two perfect bodyes are incorporate,
His life holdes mine, his heart conteines my hart,
His euery lim, containes my euery part :
Without his being, I can neuer be,
He being dead, prepare to burie me.
Oh thou immortall mouer of the spheares,
Within their circled reuolusions,
Whose glorious image this small orphant beares,
Wrought by thy all sufficient Maiestie,
Oh neuer suffer any wicked hand,
To harme this heauenly workmanship of thine,
But let him liue, great God to honour thee,
With vertuous life, and spotlesse pietie.

Per. Cease my kinde cooze, I cannot choose but weepe,
To see your care of my securitie.

Allen. Knewst thou my reason, that perswades my hart,
Thou wouldst not wonder, why I grieue to part :
But yet I would suspect my fathers vowe,
Did any other make it by your leaue.

Fall. What haue you done, this lothnesse to depart,
Seemes you were trained vp in tediousnesse,
That know not when and where to make an end:
Take him my friends, I know you will discharge,
The hope and trust that I repose in you.

Both. Assure your selfe, in euery circumstance.

Fall. Then to your horses, quicklie, speedily,
Else we shall put our fingers in the eye,
And weepe for kindnesse till to morrow morne.

Per, Farewell good Vnckle, Aunt, and louing cooze.

        Sostratus kisseth the boy weeping.

Allen, Farewell, I feare me euerlastinglie.

        Exeunt Sostratus *and* Allenso.
      One of the murtherers takes Falleria *by the*
         sleeue.

1. mu. You meane not now to haue him murthered?

Fall. Not murthered, what else? kill him I say,
But wherefore makest thou question of my will?

                    Mur.

Mur. Becaufe you wifht that God fhould be reueng'd
If any ill betide the innocent.

Fall. Oh that was nothing but to blind the eyes,
Of my fond fonne, which loues him too too well.

Mur. It is enough, it fhall be furely done. *Exeunt om.*

Enter Merry *and* Rachel *with a bag.*

Mer. What haft thou fped ? haue you bought the bag?

Rach. I brother, here it is, what is't to do ?

Mer. To beare hence *Beeches* body in the night.

Rach. You cannot beare fo great a waight your felfe,
And 'tis no trufting of another man.

Mer. Yes well enough, as I will order it,
Ile cut him peece-meale, firft his head and legs
Will be one burthen, then the mangled reft,
Will be another, which I will tranfport,
Beyond the water in a Ferry boate,
And throw it into *Paris-garden* ditch,
Fetch me the chopping-knife, and in the meane
Ile moue the Fagots that do couer him.
               Remooue the Fagots.

Rach. Oh can you finde in hart to cut and carue,
His ftone colde flefh, and rob the greedy graue,
Of his diffeuered blood befprinckled lims ?

Mer. I mary can I fetch the chopping knife.

Rach. This deed is worfe, the whe you tooke his life. *Exit*

Mer. But worfe, or better, now it muft be fo,
Better do thus, then feele a greater woe.

Ent. Rach. Here is the knife, I cannot ftay to fee,
This barbarous deed of inhumanitie.   *Exit Rachel.*

          Merry *begins to cut the body , and bindes the armes*
               behinde his backe with Beeches *garters, leaues*
               out the body, couers the head and legs againe.

Enter Truth.

Yee glorious beames of that bright-fhining lampe,
That lights the ftarre befpangled firmament,

               E 2   And

And dimnes the glimmering shadowes of the night,
Why doost thou lend assistance to this wretch,
To shamble forth with bolde audacitie,
His lims, that beares thy makers semblance.
All you the sad spectators of this Acte,
Whose harts do taste a feeling pensiuenesse,
Of this vnheard of sauadge Massacre :
Oh be farre of, to harbour such a thought,
As this audacious murtherer put in vre,
I see your sorrowes flowe vp to the brim,
And ouerflowe your cheekes with brinish teares,
But though this sight bring surfet to the eye,
Delight your eares with pleasing harmonie,
That eares may counterchecke your eyes, and say,
Why shed you teares, this deede is but a playe :
His worke is done, he seekes to hide his sinne,
Ile waile his woe, before his woe begin.   *Exit* Trueth.
  Mer. Now will I high me to the water side,
And fling this heauie burthen in a ditche,
Whereof my soule doth feele so great a waight,
That it doth almost presse me downe with feare,
                              Enter Rachell.
Harke *Rachel* : I will crosse the water straight,
And fling this middle mention of a man,
Into some ditch, then high me home againe,
To rid my house of that is left behinde.
  Rach. Where haue you laide the legs & battered head?
  Mer. Vnder the fagots, where it lay before,
Helpe me to put this trunke into the bag.
  Rach. My heart will not endure to handle it,
The sight hereof doth make me quake for feare.
  Mer. Ile do't my selfe, onely drie vp the blood,
And burne the clothes as you haue done before.   *Exit.*
  Rach. I feare thy soule will burne in flames of hell,
Vnlesse repentance wash away thy sinne,
With clensing teares of true contrition :
Ah did not nature ouersway my will,

                                                    The

The world should know this plot of damned ill.   *Exit*

Enter two Murtherers with Pertillo.

Per. I am so wearie in this combrous wood,
That I must needes go sit me downe and rest.

   1. Mur. What were we best to kill him vnawares,
Or giue him notice what we doe intend?

   2. Mur. Whie then belike you meane to do your charge
And feele no tast of pittie in your hart.

   1. Mur Of pittie man, that neuer enters heere,
And if it should, Ide threat my crauen hart,
To stab it home, for harbouring such a thought,
I see no reason whie I should relent:
It is a charitable vertuous deede,
To end this princkocke from this sinfull world.

   2. Mur. Such charitie will neuer haue reward,
Vnlesse it be with sting of conscience:
And that's a torment worse then *Sisipus*,
That rowles a restlesse stone against the hill.

   1. Mur. My conscience is not prickt with such conceit.

   2. Mur. That shews thee further off from hoped grace.

   1. Mur. Grace me no graces, I respect no grace,
But with a grace, to giue a gracelesse stab,
To chop folkes legges and armes off by the stumpes,
To see what shift theile make to scramble home:
Pick out mens eyes, and tell them thats the sport,
Of hood-man-blinde, without all sportiuenesse,
If with a grace I can performe such pranckes,
My hart will giue mine agents many thankes.

   2. Mur. Then God forbid I should consort my selfe,
With one so far from grace and pietie:
Least being found within thy companie,
I should be partner of thy punishment.

   1. Mur. When wee haue done what we haue vow'd to
My hart desires to haue no fellowship,   (do,
With those that talke of grace or godlinesse:
I nam'd not God vnleast twere with an othe,
Sence the first houre that I could walke alone,

E 3   (And

(And you that make so much of conscience,
By heauen thou art a damned hipocrite:
For thou hast vow'd to kill that sleeping boy,   1290
And all to gaine two hundreth markes in gold,
I know this purenesse comes of pure deceit,
To draw me from the murthering of the child,
That you alone might haue the benefit,
You are too shallow, if you gull me so,
Chop of my head to make a Sowsing-tub,
And fill it full of tripes and chitterlinges.

   2. Mur. That thou shalt see my hart is far from fraud,
Or vaine illusion in this enterprize,   1300
Which doth import the safetie of our soules,
There take my earnest of impietie.   *Giue him his mony.*
Onely forbeare to lay thy ruder handes,
Vpon the poore mistrustlesse tender child,
As for our vowes, feare not their violence,
God will forgiue on hartie penitence.

   1. Mur. Thou Eunuch, Capon, dastard, fast and loose,
Thou weathercocke of mutabilitie,
White liuered Paisant, wilt thou vowe and sweare,
Face and make semblance with thy bagpipe othes,   1310
Of that thou neuer meanst to execute ?
Pure cowardice for feare to crack thy necke,
With the huge *Caos* of thy bodies waight,
Hath sure begot this true contrition,
Then fast and pray, and see if thou canst winne,
A goodlie pardon for thy hainous sinne,
As for the boy, this fatall instrument,
Was mark'd by heauen to cut his line of life,
And must supplie the knife of *Atropos*,
And if it doe not, let this maister peece,   1320
(Which nature lent the world to wonder at)
Be slit in *Carbonadoes* for the iawes,
Of some men-eating hungrie *Canniball*:
By heauen ile kill him onely for this cause,
For that he came of vertuous Auncestors,

                                                  2. m. But

2.m. But by that God, which made that wondrous globe,
Wherein is seene his powerfull dietie,
Thou shalt not kill him maugre all thy spight:
Sweare, and forsweare thy selfe ten thousand times,
Awake *Pertillo*, for thou art betrai'd,
This bloody slaue intends to murther thee.　　*Draw both.*
　1.mur. Both him, and all, that dare to rescue him.
　Per. Wherefore? because I slept without your leaue?
Forgiue my fault, Ile neuer sleepe againe.
　2.mur. No child, thy wicked Vnckle hath suborn'd,
Both him and me to take thy life away:
Which I would saue, but that this hellish impe,
Will not consent to spare thy guiltlesse blood.
　Per. Why should *Falleria* seeke to haue my life.
　2.mur. The lands and goods, thy father left his sonne,
Do hale thee on to thy destruction.
　Per. Oh needy treasure, harme begetting good,
That safely should procure the losse of blood.
　2.mu. Those lands and goods, thy father got with paine,
Are swords wherewith his little sonne is slaine.
　1.mu. Then let our swords let out his guitlesse life.
　Per. Sweete, sowre, kinde, cruell, holde thy murthering
And here me speake, before you murther me.　　(knife,
　2.mu. Feare not sweet child, he shall not murther thee.
　1.mu. No, but my sword shall let his puddings foorth.
　Per. First here me speake, thou map of Butcherie,
Tis but my goods and lands my Vnckle seekes,
Hauing that safely, he desires no more,
I do protest by my dead parents soules,
By the deare loue of false *Fallerios* sonne,
Whose heart, my heart assures me, will be grieu'd,
To heare his fathers inhumanitie:
I will forsake my countrie, goods, and lands,
I and my selfe, will euen change my selfe,
In name, in life, in habit, and in all,
And liue in some farre moued continent,
So you will spare my weake and tender youth,
　　　　　　　　　　　　　　　Which

Which cannot entertaine the ftroake of death,
In budding yeares, and verie fpring of life.

 1.Mur. Leaue of thefe bootlefle proteftations,
And vfe no ruth entifing argumentes,
For if you doe, ile lop you lim by lim,
And torture you for childifh eloquence.

  2.Mur. Thou fhalt not make his little finger ake.

  1.Mur. Yes euery part, and this fhall prooue it true.

   Runnes Pertillo *in with his fworde.*   1370

 Per. Oh I am flaine, the Lord forgiue thy fact,
And giue thee grace to dye with penitence.   *Dyeth.*

  2.Mur. A treacherous villaine, full of cowardife,
Ile make thee know that thou haft done amifle.

  1.m. Teach me that knowledge when you will or dare.

   They fight and kill one another, the relenter hauing
   fome more life, and the other dyeth.

  1. mur. Swoones I am peppered, I had need haue falt,
Or elfe to morrow I fhall yeeld a ftincke,   1380
Worfe then a heape of durty excrements :
Now by this Hilt, this golde was earn'd too deare :
Ah, how now death, wilt thou be conquerour ?
Then vengeance light on them that made me fo,
And ther's another farewell ere I goe.

   Stab the other murtherer againe.

  2.mur. Enough, enough, I had my death before.

   A hunt within.

  Enter the Duke of Padua, Turqualo, Vefuvio,
   Alberto, *&c.*   1390

 Duke. How now my Lords, was't not a gallant courfe,
Beleeue me firs, I neuer faw a wretch,
Make better fhift to faue her little life :
The thickets full of buskes and fcratching bryers,
A mightie dewe, a many deepe mouth'd hounds,
Let loofe in euery place to crofle their courfe,
And yet the Hare got cleanly from them all :
I would not for a hundred pound in faith,

           But

40

But that she had escaped with her life,
For we will winde a merry hunters horne,
And start her once againe to morrow morne.

   Tarq. In troth my Lord, the little flocked hound,
That had but three good legs to further him,
Twas formost still, and surer of his sent,
Then any one in all the crie besides.

   Vesu. But yet *Pendragon* gaue the Hare more turnes.

   Alber. That was becaufe he was more polliticke,
And eyed her closely in her couerts still:
They all did well, and once more we will trie,
The subtile creature with a greater crie.

          Enter Allenso *booted.*

   Duke. But say, what well accomplishd Gentleman,
Is this that comes into our company?

   Vesu. I know him well, it is *Falerios* sonne,
Pandynos brother (a kinde Gentleman)
That dyed, and left his little pretty sonne,
Vnto his fathers good direction.

   Duke. Stand close awhile, and ouer heare his wordes,
He seemes much ouer-gone with passion.

   Alen. Yee timorous thoughts that guide my giddy steps,
In vnknowne pathes of dreadfull wildernesse,
Why traitor-like do you conspire to holde,
My pained heart, twixt feare and iealousie,
My too much care hath brought me carelesly,
Into this woody sauadge labyrinth,
And I can finde no waye to issue out,
Feare hath so dazeled all my better part,
That reason hath forgot discreations art:
But in good time, see where is company.
Kinde Gentlemen, if you vnlike my selfe,
Are not incumbred with the circling wayes,
Of this erronious winding wildernesse,
I pray you to direct me foorth this wood,
And shew the pathe that leades to *Padua.*

   Duke. We all are *Paduans,* and we all intend,

F   To

To passe forthwith, with speed to *Padua*.
 Allen. I will attend vpon you presently. *See the bodyes.*
 Duke. Come then away, but gentlemen beholde,
A bloody sight, and murtherous spectacle.
 2. Mur. Oh God forgiue me all my wickednesse,
And take me to eternall happinesse.

 Duke. Harke one of them hath some small sparke of life, 1440
To kindle knowledge of their sad mishaps.

 Alen. Ah gratious Lord, I know this wretched child,
And these two men that here lye murthered.
 Vesu. Do you *Alenso*? *Allen*. I my gratious Lord:
It was *Pertillo* my dead Vnckles sonne :
Now haue my feares brought forth this fearefull childe,
Of endlesse care, and euerlasting griefe.

 Duke. Lay hands vpon *Alenso* Gentlemen, 1450
Your presence doth confirme you had a share,
In the performance of this crueltie.

 Alen. I do confesse I haue so great a share,
In this mishap, that I will giue him thankes,
That will let foorth my sorrow wounded soule,
From out this goale of lamentation.

 Duke. Tis now too late to wish for hadiwist,
Had you withheld your hand from this attempt,
Sorrow had neuer so imprisoned you.

 Allen. Oh my good Lord, you do mistake my case, 1460
And yet my griefe is sure infallible,
The Lord of heauen can witnesse with my soule,
That I am guiltlesse of your wrong suspect,
But yet not griefelesse that the deed is done.

 Duke. Nay if you stand to iustifie your selfe,
This Gentleman whose life dooth seeme to stay,
Within his body tell he tell your shame,
Shall testifie of your integritie :
Speake then thou sad Anatomy of death,
Who were the agents of your wofulnesse. 1470

 2. Mur. O be not blinded with a false surmise,
For least my tongue should faile to end the tale.

Of

Of our vntimely fate appointed death :
Know young *Allenso* is as innocent,
As is *Fallerio* guiltie of the crime.
He, he it was, that with foure hundreth markes,
Whereof two hundred he paide presently,
Did hire this damn'd villaine and my selfe,
To massacre this harmelesse innocent:
But yet my conscience toucht with some remorse,
Would faine haue sau'd the young *Pertilos* life,
But he remorselesse would not let him liue,
But vnawares thrust in his harmlesse brest,
That life bereauing fatall instrument :
Which cruell deede I seeking to reuenge,
Haue lost my life, and paid the slaue his due
Rewarde, for spilling blood of Innocents :
Surprise *Fallerio* author of this ill,
Saue young *Allenso*, he is guiltlesse still.   *Dyeth.*

   Allen. Oh sweetest honie mixt with bitter gall,
Oh Nightingale combinde with Rauens notes,
Thy speech is like a woodward that should say,
Let the tree liue, but take the roote away.
As though my life were ought but miserie,
Hauing my father slaine for infamie.

   Duke. What should incite *Fallerio* to deuise,
The ouerthrowe of this vnhappie boy.

   Vesu. That may be easily guest my gracious Lord,
To be the lands *Pandino* left his sonne,
Which after that the boy were murthered,
Discend to him by due inheritance.

   Duke. You deeme aright, see gentlemen the fruites,
Of coueting to haue anothers right,
Oh wicked thought of greedie couetice,
Could neither nature, feare of punishment,
Scandall to wife and children, nor the feare,
Of Gods confounding strict seueritie,
Allay the head-strong furie of thy will,
Beware my friends to wish vnlawfull gaine,

         It

It will beget strange actions full of feare, 1510
And ouerthrowe the actor vnawares,
For first *Fallerios* life must satiffie,
The large effusion of their guiltlesse bloods,
Traind on by him to these extremities,
Next, wife and children must be dispofest,
Of lands and goods, and turnde to beggerie,
But most of all, his great and hainous sinne,
Will be an eye sore to his guiltlesse kinne.
Beare hence away these models of his shame, 1520
And let vs profecute the murtherer,
With all the care and dilligence we can.

         Two must be carrying away Pertillo.

  Allen. Forbeare a while, to beare away my ioy,
Which now is vanisht, since his life is fled,
And giue me leaue to wash his deadly wound,
With hartie teares, out-flowing from those eyes,
Which lou'd his sight, more then the sight of heauen:
Forgiue me God for this idolatrie.
Thou vgly monster, grim imperious death, 1530
Thou raw-bonde lumpe of foule deformitie.
Reguardlesse instrument of cruell fate,
Vnparciall Sergeant, full of treacherie,
Why didst thou flatter my ill boding thoughts,
And flesh my hopes with vaine illusions:
Why didst thou say, *Pertillo* should not dye,
And yet, oh yet, hast done it cruelly :
Oh but beholde, with what a smiling cheere,
He intertain'd thy bloody harbinger:
See thou transformer of a heauenly face, 1540
To Ashie palenesse and vnpleasing lookes,
That his faire countenance still reteineth grace,
Of perfect beauty in the very graue,
The world would say such beauty should not dye,
Yet like a theefe thou didst it cruelly :
Ah, had thy eyes deepe sunke into thy head,
Beene able to perceiue his vertuous minde,

                       Where

Where vertue sate inthroned in a chaire,
With awfull grace, and pleasing maiestie:
Thou wouldest not then haue let *Pertillo* die,
Nor like a theefe haue slaine him cruellie.
Ineuitable fates, could you deuise,
No meanes to bring me to this pilgrimage,
Full of great woes and sad calamities,
But that the father should be principall,
To plot the present downfall of the sonne:
Come then kinde death and giue me leaue to die,
Since thou hast slaine *Pertillo* cruellie.

    Du. Forbeare *Allenso* harken to my doome,
Which doth concerne thy fathers apprehension,
First we enioyne thee vpon paine of death,
To giue no succour to thy wicked sire,
But let him perrish in his damned sinne;
And pay the price of such a trecherie:
See that with speede the monster be attach'd,
And bring him safe to suffer punishment,
Preuent it not, nor seeke not to delude,
The officers to whom this charge is giuen,
For if thou doe, as sure as God doth liue :
Thy selfe shall satisfie the lawes contempt,
Therefore forward about this punishment.

                        Exeunt omnes manet Allenso.

    Al. Thankes gratious God that thou hast left the meanes
To end my soule from this perplexitie,
Not succour him on paine of present death:
That is no paine, death is a welcome guest,
To those whose harts are ouerwhelm'd with griese,
My woes are done, I hauing leaue to die,
And after death liue euer ioyfullie.   *Exit.*

     Enter Murther and Couetousnesse.

    Mur. Now *Auarice* I haue well satisfied,
My hungry thoughtes with blood and crueltie:
Now all my melanchollie discontent,

            F 3   Is

Is shaken of, and I am throughlie pleas'd,
With what thy pollicie hath brought to passe,
Yet am I not so throughlie satisfied:
Vntill I bring the purple actors forth,
And cause them quaffe a bowle of bitternesse,
That father, sonne, and sister brother may,
Bring to their deathes with most assur'd decay.

   Aua. That wilbe done without all question,
For thou hast slaine *Allenso* with the boy:
And *Rachell* doth not wish to ouerliue,
The sad remembrance of her brothers sinne,
Leaue faithfull loue, to teach them how to dye,
That they may share their kinsfolkes miserie.   *Exeunt.*

Enter Merrie *and* Rachell *vncouering the*
head and legges.

   Mer. I haue bestow'd a watrie funerall,
On the halfe bodie of my butchered friend,
The head and legges Ile leaue in some darke place,
I care not if they finde them yea or no.

   Ra. Where do you meane to leaue the head and legs,

   Mer. In some darke place nere to Bainardes castle,

   Ra. But doe it closelie that you be not seene,
For all this while you are without suspect.

   Mer. Take you no thought, ile haue a care of that,
Onelie take heede you haue a speciall care,
To make no shew of any discontent,
Nor vse too many words to any one.
               Puts on his cloake taketh vp the bag.
I will returne when I haue left my loade,
Be merrie *Rachell* halfe the feare is past.

   Ra. But I shall neuer thinke my selfe secure,   *Exit.*
This deede would trouble any quiet soule,
To thinke thereof, much more to see it done,
Such cruell deedes can neuer long be hid,
Although we practice nere so cunningly.

                                Let

Let others open what I doe conceale,
Lo he is my brother, I will couer it,
And rather dye then haue it spoken rife,
Lo where ihe goes, betrai'd her brothers life.　　*Exit.*

Enter Williams *and* Cowley.

Cō. Why how now *Harry* what fhould be the caufe,
That you are growne fo difcontent of late :
Your fighes do fhew fome inward heauineffe,
Your heauy lookes, your eyes brimfull of teares,
Beares teftimonie of fome fecret griefe,
Reueale it *Harry*, I will be thy friend,
And helpe thee to my poore habillity.

Wil. If I am heauie, if I often figh,
And if my eyes beare recordes of my woe,
Condemne me not, for I haue mightie caufe,
More then I will impart to any one.

Co. Do you mifdoubt me, that you dare not tell
That woe to me, that moues your difcontent.

Wil. Good maifter *Cowley* you were euer kinde,
But pardon me, I will not vtter it,
To any one, for I haue paft my worde,
And therefore vrge me not to tell my griefe.

Cow. But thofe that fmother griefe too fecretly,
May waft themfelues in filent anguifhment,
And bring their bodies to fo low an ebbe,
That all the world can neuer make is flowe,
Vnto the happy hight of former health:
Then be not iniurious to thy felfe,
To waft thy ftrength in lamentation,
But tell thy cafe, wele feeke fome remedie.

Wil. My caufe of griefe is now remedileffe,
And all the world can neuer leffen it,
Then fince no meanes can make my forrowes leffe,
Suffer me waile a woe which wants redreffe.

Cow. Yet let me beare a part in thy lamentes,
I loue thee not fo ill, but I will mone,

F 4　　　　　　　　　　Thy

Thy heauie haps, thou shalt not sigh alone.

Wil. Nay, if you are so curious to intrude,
Your selfe to sorrow, where you haue no share,
I will frequent some vnfrequented place,
Where none shall here nor see my lamentations.

Cow. And I will follow where soeuer thou goe,　　*Exit.*
I will be partner of thy helplesse woe.　　　　　　*Exit.*

　　　　　　　　Enter two Watermen.

1. Will ist not time we should go to our boates,
And giue attendance for this Bartlemew tide:
Folkes will be stirring early in the morning.

2. By my troth I am indifferent whether I go or no.
If a fare come why so, if not, why so, if I haue not their
money, they shall haue none of my labour.

1. But we that liue by our labours, must giue attendance,
But where lyes thy Boate?

2. At Baynards castle staires.

1. So do's mine, then lets go together.

2. Come, I am indifferent, I care not so much for going,
But if I go with you, why so: if not, why so.

　　　　　　　　　　He falles ouer the bag.
Sblood what rascall hath laide this in my way?

1. A was not very indifferent that did so, but you are so
permentorie, to say, why so, and why so, that euery one is
glad to do you iniurie, but lets see, what is it?

　　　　　　　　Taking the Sack by the end, one of the
　　　　　　　　legs and head drops out.
Good Lord deliuer vs, a mans legges, and a head with manie wounds.

2. Whats that so much, I am indifferent, yet for mine
owne part, I vnderstand the miserie of it, if you doe, why
so, if not, why so.

1. By my troth I vnderstand no other mistery but this,
It is a strange and very rufull sight,
But prethee what doost thou conceit of it.

2 In troth I am indifferent, for if I tell you, why so, if not
　　　　　　　　　　　　　　　　　　　　why

why so.

1. If thou tell me, Ile thanke thee, therefore I prithee tell me.

2. I tell you I am indifferent, but to be plaine with you, I am greeued to stumble at the hangmans budget.

1. At the hangmans budget, why this is a sack.

2. And to speake indifferently, it is the hang-mans Budget, and because he thought too much of his labour to set this head vpon the bridge, and the legs vpon the gates, he flings them in the streete for men to stumble at, but if I get him in my boate, Ile so belabour him in a stretcher, that he had better be stretcht in one of his owne halfepeny halters: if this be a good conceit, why so, if not, why so.

1. Thou art deceiu'd, this head hath many wounds, And hoase and shooes remaining on the legs, *Bull* alwayes strips all quartered traitors quite.

2. I am indifferent whether you beleeue me or no, these were not worth taking off, and therfore he left them on, if this be likely why so, if not, why so.

1. Nay then I see you growe from worse to worse, I heard last night, that one neere Lambert hill Was missing, and his boye was murthered, It may be this is a part of that same man: What ere it be, Ile beare it to that place.

2. Masse I am indifferent, Ile go along with you, If it be so, why so, if not why so.   *Exeunt.*

Enter three neighbors knocking at Loneys
doore: Loney *comes.*

1. Hoe maister *Loney,* here you any newes, What is become of your Tennant *Beech?*

Lon. No truely sir, not any newes at all.

2. What hath the boy recouered any speach, To giue vs light of these suggestions, That do arise vpon this accident.

Lon. There is no hope he should recouer speech, The wiues do say, he's ready now to leaue

G   This

This greeuous world full fraught with treacherie,

    3. Me thinkes if *Beech* himselfe be innocent,
That then the murtherer should not dwell farre off,
The hammer that is sticking in his head,
Was borrowed of a Cutler dwelling by,
But he remembers not, who borrowed it:
He is committed that did owe the hammer,
But yet hē standes vppon his innocence,
And *Beeches* absence causeth great suspition.

    Lo. If *Beech* be faulty, as I do not thinke,
I neuer was so much deceiu'd before,
Oh had you knowne his conuersation,
Yoū would not haue him in suspition.

    3. Diuels seeme Saints, and in this hatefull times,
Deceite can beare apparraunt signes of trueth,
And vice beare shew of vertues excellence.

    Enter the two VVatermen.

    1. I pray is this maister *Beeches* house?

    Lo. My friend this same was maister *Beeches* shop,
We cannot tell whether he liue or no,

    1. Know you his head and if I shew it you,
Or can you tell what hose or shooes he ware,
At that same time when he forsooke the shoppe.

    3. What haue you head, and hose, and shooes to show,
And want the body that should vse the same.

    1. Behold this head, these legges, these hose and shooes,
And see if they were *Beeches* yea or no.

    Lo. They are the same, alas what is become,
Of the remainder of this wretched man.

    1.VVat. Nay that I know not, onelie these we found,
As we were comming vp a narrow lane,
Neere Baynardes Castle, where we two did dwell,
And heering that a man was missing hence,
We thought it good to bring these to this place, (paines,

    3. Thankes my good friendes, ther's some thing for your

    2.Wat. We are indifferēt, whether you giue vs any thing
or nothing, and if you had not, why so, but since you haue,
why so.
                                    1.Wat.

1730

1740

1750

1760

1.Wat. Leaue your repining sir we thanke you hartely.
3. Farewell good fellowes, neighbour now be bold,

Exeunt Watermen.

They dwell not farre that did this bloodie deed,
As God no boubt will at the last reueale:
Though they conceale it nere so cunninglie,
All houses, gutters, sincks and creuices,
Haue carefullie beene sought for, for the blood.
Yet theres no instaunce found in any place.

Enter a Porter and a gentleman.

But who is that, that brings a heauy loade,
Behinde him on a painefull porters backe.
Gen. Praie gentlemen which call you *Beeches* shoppe?
3.Neig. This is the place, what wold you with the man?
Gen. Nothing with him, I heare the man is dead,
And if he be not, I haue lost my paines.
Lo. Hees dead indeede, but yet we cannot finde,
What is become of halfe his hopelesse bodie,
His head and legges are foind but for the rest,
No man can tell what is become of it.
Gen. Then I doe thinke I can resolue your doubt,
And bring you certaine tydings of the rest,
And if you know his doublet and his shirt:
As for the bodie it is so abus'd.
That no man can take notice whoes it was,
Set downe this burthen of anothers shame,
What do you know the doublet and the shirt. *Ex. Porter.*
Lo. This is the doublet, these the seuered limmes,
Which late were ioyned to that mangled trunke:
Lay them together see if they can make,
Among them all a sound and solid man.
3.neigh. They all agree, but yet they cannot make,
That sound and whole, which a remorsles hand
Hath seuered with a knife of crueltie:
But say good sir, where did you finde this out?
Gent. Walking betime by Paris-garden ditch,
Hauing my Water Spaniell by my side,

G 2   When

When we approach'd vnto that haplesse place,
Where this same trunke lay drowned in a ditch,
My Spaniell gan to sent, to barke, to plunge,
Into the water, and came foorth againe,
And fawnd on me, as if a man should say,
Helpe out a man that heere lyes murthered.
At first I tooke delight to see the dog,
Thinking in vaine some game did there lye hid,
Amongst the Nettles growing neere the banke:
But when no game, nor any thing appear'd,
That might produce the Spaniell to this sport,
I gan to rate and beate the harmlesse Cur,
Thinking to make him leaue to follow me,
But words, nor blowes, could mooue the dog away,
But still he plung'd, he diu'd, he barkt, he ran
Srill to my side, as if it were for helpe:
I seeing this, did make the ditch be dragd,
Where then was found this body as you see,
With great amazement to the lookers on.

   3. Beholde the mightie miracles of God,
That sencelesse things should propagate their sinne,
That are more beastiall farre then beastlinesse,
Of any creature most insensible.

   2. neigh. Cease we to wonder at Gods wondrous works,
And let vs labour for to bring to light,
Those masked fiends that thus dishonor him:
This sack is new, and loe beholde his marke
Remaines vpon it, which did sell the bag,
Amongst the Salters we shall finde it out,
When, and to whom, this bloody bag was sold.

   3. Tis very likely, let no paines be spar'd,
To bring it out, if it be possible,
Twere pitty such a murther should remaine
Vnpunished, mongst Turkes and Infidels.

   1. neigh. Sirs, I do know the man that solde this bag,
And if you please, Ile fetch him presently?
   Gent. With all our harts, how say you Gentlemen?

                      Per-

Perchance the murther thus may come to light.

    3. I pray you do it, we will tarry heere: *Exit 1.neigh.*

And let the eyes of euery paſſenger

Be ſatiſfied, which may example be,

How they commit ſo dreadfull wickedneſſe.

   Ent.wom. And pleaſe your maiſterſhips the boy is dead.

    3.neigh. Tis very ſtrange, that hauing many wounds,

So terrible, ſo ghaſtlie, which is more,

Hauing the hammer ſticking in his head,

That he ſhould liue and ſtirre from Friday night,

To Sunday morning, and euen then depart,

When that his Maiſters mangled courſe were found,

Bring him foorth too, perchance the murtherers

May haue their hearts touched with due remorſe,

Viewing their deeds of damned wickedneſſe.

        Bring forth the boye and lay him by.Beech.

  1.neigh. Here is the Salters man that ſolde the bag,

   Gent. My friend, how long ſince did you ſell that bag?

And vnto whom, if you remember it?

   Sal. I ſould the bag good ſir but yeſterday,

Vnto a maide, I do not know her name.

    3.neigh. Nor where ſhe dwels.   *Sal.* No certeinly.

    2.neigh. But what apparell had ſhe on her back?

   Sal. I do not well remember what ſhe wore,

But if I ſaw her I ſhould know her ſure.

    3.neigh. Go round about to euery neighbors houſe,

And will them ſhew their maides immediatly:

God graunt we may finde out the murtherers.

        Go to one houſe, and knock at doore, asking,

Bring forth ſuch maides as are within your houſe.

   1.houſekeeper. I haue but one, ile ſend her downe to you.

    3.neigh. Is this the maide.   *Come out maide.*

   Salt. No ſir, this is not ſhe.   *Go to another, &c.*

How many maides do dwell within this houſe?

   2.houſe. Her's nere a woman here, except my wife.

       Go to Merryes.

    3.neigh. Whoſe houſe is this?

        G 3   *Loney.*

Lon. An honeſt ciuill mans, cald *Maiſter Merry,*
Who I dare be ſworne, would neuer do ſo great a murther
But you may aske heere to for faſhion ſake.

        Rachel ſits in the ſhop.

  3. How now faire maide, dwels any here but you?
Thou haſt too true a face for ſuch a deed.

  Rach. No gentle ſir, my brother keepes no more.

  3. neigh. This is not ſhe? *Sal.* No truly gentlemā. *Ex. R.*

  3. This will not ſerue, we cannot finde her out,
Bring in thoſe bodyes, it growes towards night,
God bring theſe damn'd murtherers at length to light.

                  Exeunt omnes.

       Enter Merry *and* Rachel.

  Mer. Why go the neighbours round about the ſtreete
To euery houſe? what haſt thou heard the cauſe?

  Rach They go about with that ſame Salters man,
Of whom I bought the bag but yeſterday,
To ſee if he can know the maide againe
Which bought it, this I thinke the very cauſe.

  Mer. How were my ſences ouercome with feare,
That I could not foreſee this ieopardy:
For had I brought the bag away with me,
They had not had this meanes to finde it out.
Hide thee aboue leaſt that the Salters man,
Take notice of thee that thou art the maide,
And by that knowledge we be all vndone.

  Rach That feare is paſt, I ſawe, I ſpake with him,
Yet he denies that I did buy the bag:
Beſides, the neighbors haue no doubt of you,
Saying you are an honeſt harmeleſſe man,
And made enquirie heere for faſhion ſake.

  Mer. My former life, deſerues their good conceits,
Were it not blemiſht with this treacherie.
My heart is merier then it was before,
For now I hope the greateſt feare is paſt,
The hammer is denyed, the bag vnknowne,
Now there is left no meanes to bring it out,

                       Vnleſſe

Vnlesse our selues prooue Traitors to our selues.

   Rach. When saw you *Harry Williams*? *Me.* Why to day
I met him comming home from *Powles* Crosse,
Where he had beene to heare a Sermon.

   Rach. Why brought you not the man along with you
To come to dinner, that we might perswade
Him to continue in his secrecie.

   Mer. I did intreate him, but he would not come,
But vow'd to be as secret as my selfe.

   Rach. What, did he sweare?

   Mer. What neede you aske me that?
You know we neuer heard him sweare an othe.
But since he hath conceal'd the thing thus long,
I hope in God he will conceale it still.

   Rach. Pray God he do, and then I haue no doubt,
But God will ouerpasse this greeuous sinne,
If you lament with true vnfained teares,
And seeke to liue the remnant of your yeares,
In Gods true feare with vpright conscience.

   Mer. If it would please him pardon this amisse,
And rid my body from the open shame,
That doth attend this deed, being brought to light,
I would endeuour all my comming dayes,
To please my maker, and exalt his praise:
But it growes late, come bring me to my bed,
That I may rest my sorrow charged head.

   Rach. Rest still in calme secure tranquillitie,
And ouer-blowe this storme of mightie feare,
With pleasant gales of hoped quietnesse,
Go when you will, I will attend, and pray,
To send this wofull night a cheerefull day.   *Exeunt.*

Enter Falleria *and* Sostrata
weeping.

   Fall. Passe ore these rugged furrowes of laments,
And come to plainer pathes of cheerefulnesse,
Cease thy continuall showers of thy woe,

                    And

And let my pleasing wordes of comfort chase,
This duskie cloudes of thy vniust dispaire,
Farre from thy hart, and let a pleasing hope,
Of young *Pertillos* happy safe returne,
Establish all your ill deuining thoughts,
So shall you make me cheerefull that am sad,
And feede your hopes with fond illusions.

   Sos. I could be so, but my diuided soule,
Twixt feare and hope of young *Pertillos* life,
Cannot ariue at the desired port,
Of firme beleefe, vntill mine eyes do see,
Him that I sent to know the certainetie.

   Fal. To know the certaintie, of whom, of what,
Whome, whether, when, or whereabout I praie,
Haue you dispatcht a frustrate messenger,
By heauen, and earth, my heart misguiseth me,
They will preuent my cunning pollicie.   *To the people.*
Why speake you not what winged *Pegasus*,
Is posted for your satisfaction.

   Sos. Me thinkes my speach reueales a hidden feare,
And that feare telles me, that the childe is dead.

   Fall. By sweete S. *Andrew* and my fathers soule,
I thinke the peeuish boy be too too well:
But speake, who was your passions harbinger.

   Sos. One that did kindle my misdoubting thoughtes,
With the large flame of his timiddity.

   Fall. Oh then I know the tinder of your feare,
Was young *Allenso* your white honnie sonne:
Confusion light vpon his timerous head,
For broching this large streame of fearefulnesse,
And all the plagues that damned furies feele,
For their forepassed bold iniquities:
Afflict you both for thus preuenting me.

   Sos. Preuenting you, of what, *Fallerio* speake,
For if you doe not, my poore hart will breake.

   Fall. Why of the good that I had purposed,
To young *Pertillo*, which I would conceale,

From

From you, and him, vntill the deed were done.

 Soft. If it were good, then we affect him deare,
And would adde furtherance to your enterprise.

 Fall. I say your close ease-dropping pollicies,
Haue hindred him of greater benefits,
Then I can euer do him after this :
If he liue long, and growe to riper sinne, *To the people*
Heele cursse you both, that thus haue hindered
His freedome from this goale of sinfull flesh :
But let that passe, when went your harebrainde sonne,
That Cuckow vertue-singing, hatefull byrde,
To guarde the safetie of his better part,
Which he hath pend within the childish coope,
Of young *Pertillos* sweete securitie.

 Soft. That louely sonne, that comfort of my life,
That roote of vertuous magnamitie,
That doth affect with an vnfained loue,
That tender boy, which vnder heauens bright eye,
Deserueth most to be affected deare,
Went some two houres after the little boy
Was sent away, to keepe at *Padua.*

 Fall. What is a louelie? he's a loathsome toade,
A one eyde *Cyclops,* a stigmaticke brat,
That durst attempt to contradict my will,
And prie into my close intendements.

   Enter Alenso *sad.*
Mas here a comes, his downcast sullen looke,
Is ouer waigh'd with mightie discontent,
I hope the brat is posted to his sire,
That he is growne so lazie of his pace:
Forgetfull of his dutie, and his tongue,
Is euen fast tyde with strings of heauinesse.
Come hether boye, sawst thou my obstacle,
That little *Dromus* that crept into my sonne,
With friendly hand, remoou'd and thrust away,
Say I, and please me with the sweetest note,
That euer relisht in a mortals mouth.

   H   *Alen.*

Allen. I am a Swan that singe before I dye,
Your note of shame and comming miserie.

Fall. Speake softly sonne, let not thy mother heare,
She was almost dead before for very feare.

Alen. Would I could roare as instruments of warre,
Wall battring Cannons, when the Gun-powder
Is toucht with part of *Etnas* Element,
Would I could bellow like enraged Buls,
Whose harts are full of indignation,
To be captiu'd by humaine pollicie :
Would I could thunder like Almightie *Ioue*,
That sends his farre-heard voice to terrifie,
The wicked hearts of earthly cittizens :
Then roaring, bellowing, thundring, I would say,
Mother lament, *Pertillos* made away.

Soft. What is he dead, God giue me leaue to die,
And him repentance for his treacherie.

Falleth downe and dyeth.

Fall. Neuer the like impietie was done,
A mother slaine, with terror of the sonne:
Helpe to repaire the damadge thou hast made,
And seeke to call back life with dilligence.

Allen. Call back a happie creature to more woe,
That were a sinne, good Father let her go :
O happy I, if my tormenting smart,
Could rend like her's, my griefe afflicted heart,
Would your hard hart extend vnto your wife,
To make her liue an euerdying life.
What is she dead ? oh then thrice happy she,
Whose eyes are bard from our callamitie.

Fall. I all too soone, thou viper, paracide,
But for thy tongue thy mother had not dyde,
That belching voyce, that harsh night-rauen sound,
Vntimely sent thy mother to the ground,
Vpbraid my fault, I did deceiue my brother,
Cut out thy tongue, that slue thy carefull mother.

Allen. God loue my soule, as I in heart reioyce,

To

2030

2040

2050

To haue such power in my death bringing voice,
See how in steade of teares and hartie sighes:
Of foulded armes and sorrow speaking lookes,
I doe behold with cheerefull countenance,
The liuelesse roote of my natiuitie:
And thanke her hasty soule that thence did goe,
To keepe her from het sonne and husbandes woe.
Now father giue attention to my tale:
I will not dip my griefe deciphering tongue,
In bitter wordes of reprehension,
Your deeds haue throwne more mischiefes on your head
Then wit or reason can remoue againe;
For to be briefe, *Pertillo*, oh that name
Cannot be nam'de without a hearty sigh,
Is murthered, and,   *Fal.* What and, this newes is good.
    Allen. The men which you suborn'd to murther him.
    Fal. Better and better, then it cannot out,
Vnlesse your loue will be so scripulous,
That it will ouerthrowe your selfe and me.
    Allen. The best is last, and yet you hinder me,
The Duke of *Padua* hunting in the wood:
Accompanied with Lordes and gentlemen,
    Fal. Swones what of that? what good can come of that?
    Allen. Was made acquainted by the one of them,
(That had some little remnant of his life:)
With all your practice and conspiracie?
    Fall. I would that remnant had fled quicke to hell,
To fetch fierce findes to rend their carcases,
Rather then bring my life in ieopardie :
Is this the best, swones doe you mocke me sonne,
And make a iest at my calamitie.
    Allen. Not I good father, I will ease your woe,
If you but yeeld vnto my pollicie.
    Fal. Declare it then, my wits are now to seeke,
That peece of life hath so confounded mee,
That I am wholly ouercome with feare.
    Allen. The duke hath vow'd to prosecute your life,

H 2   With

59

With all the strict seueritie he can,
But I will crosse his resolusion:
And keepe you from his furie well enough,
Ile weare your habit, I will seeme the man,
That did suborne the bloodie murtherers,
I will not stir from out this house of woe,
But waight the comming of the officers,
And answere for you fore the angrie Duke,
And if neede be suffer your punishment.

   Fall. Ile none of that, I do not like the last,
I loue thee dearer then I doe my life,
And all I did, was to aduance thy state,
To sunne bright beames of shining happinesse.

   Allen. Doubte not my life, for when I doe appeare
Before the duke, I being not the man,
He can inflict no punishment on mee.

   Fall. Mas thou saiest true, a cannot punish thee,
Thou wert no actor of their Tragædie:
But for my beard thou canst not counterfet,
And bring gray haires vppon thy downy chinne,
White frostes are neuer seene in summers spring.

   Allen. I bought a beard this day at *Padua*,
Such as our common actors vse to weare:
When youth would put on ages countenaunce,
So like in shape, in colour, and in all,
To that which growes vpon your aged face,
That were I dressed in your abilimentes,
Your selfe would scarcely know me from your selfe.

   Fal. That's excellent, what shape hast thou deuis'd,
To be my vizard to delude the worlde.

   Allen. Why thus, ile presentlie shaue off your haire,
And dresse you in a lowlie shepheardes weede,
Then you will seeme to haue the carefull charge,
Of some wealth bringing rich and fleecy flocke,
And so passe currant from suspition.

   Fall. This care of thine my sonne doth testifie,
Nature in thee hath firme predominance,

That

2100

2110

2120

2130

That neither losse of friend, nor vile reproch,
Can shake thee with their strongest violence:
In this disguise, ile see the end of thee,
That thou acquited, then maist succour me.

    Allen. I am assur'd to be exempt from woe.   *People.*
This pl... will worke my certaine ouerthrow.

    Fall. I will beare hence thy mother, and my wife,
Vntimely murthered with true sorrowes knife.   *Exit.*

    Allen. Vntimely murthered, happy was that griefe,
Which hath abridg'd whole numbers, numberlesse;
Of hart surcharging deplorations.
She shall haue due and christian funerall,
And rest in peace amongst her auncestors,
As for our bodies, they shall be inter'd,
In rauening mawes, of Rauens, Puttockes, Crowes,
Of tatlin Magpies, and deathes harbingers,
That wilbe glutted with winde shaken limmes,
Of blood delighting hate full murtherers:
And yet these many winged sepulchers,
Shall turne to earth so I, and father shall,
At last attaine to earth by funerall,
Well I will prosecute my pollicy,
That wished death may end my miseries.   *Exit*

Enter Cowley, *and* Williams.

    Cow. Still in your dumpes, good *Harry* yet at last,
Vtter your motiue of this heauinesse:
Why go you not vnto your maisters house?
What are you parted? if that be the cause,
I will prouide you of a better place.

    Wil. Who roues all day, at length may hit the marke,
That is the cause, because I cannot stay,
With him whose loue, is dearer then my life.

    Cow. Why fell you out? why did you part so soone?

    Wil. We fell not out, but feare hath parted vs.

    Cow. What did he feare your truth or honest life?

    Wil. No, no, your vnderstanding is but dimme,   *That*

H 3

That farre remooued, cannot iudge the feare,
We both were fearefull, and we both did part,
Because indeed we both were timerous.

    Cow. What accident begot your mutuall feare?
    VVil. That which my hart hath promis'd to conceale.
    Cow. Why now you fall into your auncient vaine.
    VVil. Tis vaine to vrge me from this silent vaine,
I will conceale it, though it breed my paine.

    Cow. It seemes to be a thing of consequence,
And therefore prithie *Harry* for my loue,
Open this close fast clasped mysterie.

    VVil. Were I assur'd my heart should haue release,
Of secret torment, and distemperature,
I would reueale it to you specially,
Whom I haue found my faithfull fauorite.

    Cow. Good *Harrie VVilliams* make no doubt of that,
Besides, your griefe reueal'd may haue reliefe,
Beyond your present expectation :
Then tell it *Harry*, what soere it be,
And ease your hart of horror, me of doubt.

    VVil. What haue you heard of *Beech* of Lambert hill ?
And of his boy which late were murthered.

    Cow. I heard, and sawe, their mangled carcases.
    VVil. But haue you heard of them that murthered them?
    Cow. No, would I had, for then Ide blase their shame,
And make them pay due penance for their sinne.

    VVil. This I misdoubted, therefore will forbeare,
To vtter what I thought to haue reueald.

    Cow. Knowst thou the actors of this murthrous deed,
And wilt conceale it now the deed is done?
Alas poore man, thou knowest not what thou doost,
Thou hast incur'd the danger of the lawe,
And thou mongst them must suffer punishment,
Vnlesse thou do confesse it presentlie.

    VVil. What? shall I then betray my maisters life?
    Cow. Better then hazard both thy life and soule,
To boulster out such barbarous villanie.

                    Why

2170

2180

2190

2200

Why then belike your maifter did the deed.

   VVil. My maifter vnawares efcapt my mouth,
But what the Lord doth pleafe fhall come to light,
Cannot be hid by humaine pollicie :
His haplefle hand hath wrought the fatall end,
Of *Robert Beech* and *Thomas VVinchefter.*

   Cow. Could he alone do both thofe men to death?
Hadft thou no fhare in execution?

   VVil Nor knew not of it, till the deed was done.

   Cow. If this be true, thou maift efcape with life:
Confeffe the truth vnto the officers,
And thou fhalt finde the fauour of the lawe.

   VVil. If I offended,'twas my Maifters loue,
That made me hide his great tranfgreffions:
But I will be directed as you pleafe,
So faue me God, as I am innocent.   *Exeunt.*

   Enter Alenfo *in* Falleriaes *apparrell and berd*, Falleria
fhauen in fhepheards habilliments.

   Fal. Part of my felfe, now feemft thou wholy me,
And I feeme neither like my felfe, nor thee :
Thankes to thy care, and this vnknowne difguife.
I like a fhepheard now muft learne to know,
When to lead foorth my little bleating flock,
To pleafing paftures, and well fatting walkes,
In ftormie time to driue them to the lee,
To cheere the pretie Lambes, whofe bleating voice,
Doth craue the wifhed comfort of their dams,
To found my merry Bag-pipe on the downes,
In fhearing times poore fhepheards feftiuals,
And laftlie, how to driue the Wolfe away,
That feeke to make the little Lambes their pray.

   Allen. Ah haue you care to driue the Wolfe away,
From fillie creatures wanting intellecte,
And yet would fuffer your deuouring thoughts,
To fuck the blood of your dead brothers fonne,

                                 As

As pure and innocent as any lambe,
Pertillo was, which you haue fed vpon,
But things paſt helpe may better be bewaild
With carefull teares, then finde a remedie,
Therefore for feare our practiſe be eſpide,
Let vs to queſtion of our husbandrie,
How many Lambes fell from the middle flock,
Since I my ſelfe did take the latter view.

        Enter Veſuuio, Turqual. Alberto.

  Fall. Some viue and twenty, whereof two are dead,   2250
But three and twenty ſcud about the fields,
That glads my hart to ze their iollitie.
  Veſu. This is the man, conferring of his Lambes,
That ſlew a Lambe worth all his flock beſides,
  Alen. When is the time to let the Weathers blood,
The forward ſpring, that had ſuch ſtore of graſſe,
Hath fild them full of ranke vnwholſome blood,
Which muſt be purg'd, elſe when the winter comes,
The rot will leaue me nothing but their skinnes.
  Fall. Chil let om blood, but yet it is no time,   2260
Vntill the zygne be gone below the hart.
  Veſu. Forbeare a while this idle buſineſſe,
And talke of matters of more conſequence.
  Fall. Che tell you plaine, you are no honeſt man,
To call a ſhepheards care an idle toye,
What though we haue a little merry ſport,
With flowrie gyrlonds, and an Oaten pipe,
And iolly friskins on a holly-day,
Yet is a ſhepheards cure, a greater carke,
Then ſweating Plough-men with their buſie warke.   2270
  Veſu. Hence leaue your ſheepiſh ceremoniall,
And now *Fallerio*, in the Princes name,
I do arreſt you, for the cruell murther
Of young *Pertillo* left vnto your charge,
Which you diſcharged with a bloody writ,
Sign'd by the hands of thoſe you did ſuborne:
Nay looke not ſtrange, we haue ſuch euidence,

                                  To

To ratifie your Stigian cruelty,
That cannot be deluded any way:

Allen. Alas my Lords, I know not what you say,
As for my Nephew, he I hope is well,
I sent him yesterday to *Padua.*

Alber. I, he is well, in such a vengers handes,
As will not winck at your iniquity.

Allen. By heauen and earth my soule is innocent,
Say what you will, I know my conscience.

Fal. To be afflicted with a scourge of care,
Which my oreweaning rashnesse did insflict.

Turq. Come beare him hence, expostulate no more,
That heart that could inuent such treachery,
Can teach his face to braue it cunninglie.

Alen. I do defie your accusations,
Let me haue iustice I will answere it.

Vesuu. So beare him hence, I meane to stay behinde,
To take possession of his goods and landes:
For the Dukes vse, it is too manifest.

Allen. I hope youle answere any thing you doe,
My Lord *Vesuuio* you shall answere it:
And all the rest that vse extremities.

Alber. I to the Dukes Exchecker not to you.

Exeunt omnes manet Falleria.

Fal. Thus shades are caught when substances are fled,
Indeede they haue my garments, but my selfe,
Am close enough from their discouerie,
But not so close but that my verie soule,
Is ract with tormentes for *Pertillos* death;
I am *Actern,* I doe beare about
My hornes of shame and inhumanitie,
My thoughts, like hounds which late did flatter me:
With hope of great succeeding benefits.
Now gin to teare my care-tormented heart,
With feare of death and tortring punishment,
These are the stings when as our consciences,
Are stuf'd and clogd with close concealed crimes,

I   Well

65

Well I muſt ſmoather all theſe diſcontentes,
And ſtriue to beare a ſmoother countenaunce:
Then rugged care would willingly permit,
Ile to the Court to ſee *Allenſo* free,
That he may then relieue my pouertie.　　　　*Exit.*

Enter Conſtable, three watchmen with
Halberdes.　　　　　　　　　　2320

Con. Who would haue thought of all the men aliue,
That *Thomas Merry* would haue done this deede:
So full of ruth and monſtrous wickedneſſe.

1.wat. Of all the men that liue in London walles.
I would haue thought that *Merry* had bin free,

2.wat. Is this the fruites of Saint-like Puritans,
I neuer like ſuch damn'd hipocriſie.

3.wat. He would not loaie a ſermon for a pound,　　2330
An oath he thought would rend his iawes in twaine,
An idle word did whet Gods vengeance on:
And yet two murthers were not ſcripulous,
Such cloſe illuſions God will bring to light,
And ouerthrowe the workers with his might.

Con. This is the houſe, come let vs knocke at dore,
I ſee a light they are not all in bed:

Knockes, Rachell *comes downe.*
How now faire maide, is your brother vp?

Rach. He's not within ſir, would you ſpeake with him?

Cou. You doe but ieſt, I know he is within,　　2340
And I muſt needes go vppe and ſpeake with him.

Rach. In deede good ſir, he is in bed aſleepe,
And I was loath to trouble him to night.

Con. Well ſiſter, I am ſorry for your ſake,
But for your brother, he is knowne to be
A damned villaine and an hipocrite,
Rachell, I charge thee in her highneſſe name,
To go with vs to priſon preſently.

Rach. To priſon ſir, alas what haue I done?

Con. You know that beſt, but euery one doe know,　　2350

You

66

You and your brother murthered maifter *Beech*,
And his poore boy that dwelt at Lambert hill.

   Rach. I murthered, my brother knowes that I
Did not confent to either of their deathes.

   Con. That muft be tride, where doth your brother lye?

   Rach. Here in his bed, me thinks he's not a fleepe.

   Con. Now maifter *Merry*, are you in a fweate.

                  Throwes his night cap away.

   Merry figh. No verily, I am not in a fweate.

   Con. Some fodaine feare affrights you, whats the caufe?

   Mer. Nothing but that you wak'd me vnawares.

   Con. In the Queenes name I doe commaund you rife,
And prefently to goe along with vs,   *Rifeth vp.*

   Mer. With all my hart, what doe you know the caufe?

   Con. We partly doe, when faw you maifter *Beech*?

   Mer. I doe not well remember who you meane.

   Con. Not *Beech* the chaundler vpon Lambert hill.

   Mer. I know the man, but faw him not this fortnight.

   Con. I would you had not, for your fifters fake,
For yours, for his, and for his harmeleffe boy,
Be not obdurate in your wickedneffe,
Confeffion drawes repentance after it.

   Mer. Well maifter Conftable I doe confeffe,
I was the man that did them both to death:
As for my fifter and my harmeleffe man,
I doe proteft they both are innocent.

   Con. Your man is faft in hold, and hath confeft,
The manner how, and where, the deede was done:
Therefore twere vaine to colour any thing,
Bring them away.   *Rach.* Ah brother woe is me,

   Mer. I comfortleffe will helpe to comfort thee. *Exeunt.*

           Enter Trueth.

Weepe, weepe poore foules, & enterchange your woes,
Now *Merry* change thy name and countenance:
Smile not, thou wretched creature, leaft in fcorne,
Thou fmile to thinke on thy extremities,

              I 2   Thy

Thy woes were countlesse for thy wicked deedes,
Thy sisters death neede not increase the coumpt,
For thou couldst neuer number them before :
Gentles helpe out with this suppose I pray,
And thinke it truth for Truth dooth tell the tale.
Merry by lawe conuict, as principall,
Receiues his doome, to hang till he be dead,
And afterwards for to be hangd in chaines:
Williams and *Rachell* likewise are conuict
For their concealement, *Williams* craues his booke,
And so receaues a brond of infamie.
But wretched *Rachels* sexe denies that grace,
And therefore dooth receiue a doome of death,
To dye with him, whose sinnes she did conceale.
Your eyes shall witnesse of their shaded tipes,
Which many heere did see perform'd indeed:
As for *Fallerio*, not his homelie weedes,
His beardlesse face, nor counterfetted speech,
Can shield him from deserued punishment :
But what he thinkes shall rid him from suspect ,
Shall drench him in more waues of wretchednesse,
Pulling his sonne into relentlesse iawes,
Of hungrie death, on tree of infamie :
Heere comes the Duke that doomes them both to die,
Next *Merries* death shall end this Tragedie.   *Exit.*

Enter Duke, Vesuuio, Turq. Alberto:
and Fallerio *disguised.*

Duke. Where is that *Syren*, that incarnate fiend,
Monster of Nature, spectacle of shame,
Blot and confusion of his familie,
False seeming semblance of true-dealing trust,
I meane *Fallerio* bloody murtherer:
Hath he confest his cursed treacherie,
Or will he stand to prooue his innocence.
    Vesu. We haue attach'de *Fallerio* gracious Lord,
And did accuse him with *Pertillos* death :

But

But he remote, will not confesse himselfe,
Neither the meanes, nor author of the same,
His mightie vowes and protestations,
Do almost seeme to pleade integritie,
But that we all do know the contrarie.

Fall. I know your error stricks your knowledge blinde,
His seeming me, doth so delude your minde. *People.*

Duke. Then bring him forth, to answer for himselfe,
Since he stands stoutly to denie the deed:

Alberto and other fetch Alenso.

His sonne can witnesse, that the dying man,
Accusde *Fallerio* for his treacherie.
Stand forth thou close disguised hipocrite,
And speake direttlie to these articles,
First, didst thou hire two bloodie murtherers
To massacre *Pertillo* in a wood?

Alen. I neuer did suborne such murtherers,
But euer lou'd *Pertillo* as my life:

Duke. Thy sonne can witnesse to the contrarie.

Alen. I haue no sonne to testifie so much.

Fal. No, for his grauitie is counterfeit,
Pluck of his beard, and you will sweare it so.

Vesu. Haue you no sonne? doth not *Alenso* liue?

Alen. *Alenso* liues, but is no sonne of mine.

Alber. Indeed his better part had not his source,
From thy corrupted vice affecting hart,
For vertue is the marke he aimeth at.

Duke. I dare be sworne that *Sostrata* would blush,
Shouldst thou deny *Alenso* for thy sonne.

Alen. Nay did she liue, she would not challenge me,
To be the father of that haplesse sonne.

Turq. Nay, then anon you will denie your selfe,
To be your selfe, vniust *Fallerio.*

Alen. I do confesse my selfe, to be my selfe,
But will not answere to *Fallerio.*

Duke. Not to *Fallerio*, this is excellent,
You are the man was cal'd *Fallerio.*

I 3.

Alen.

Alen. He neuer breathed yet that cal'd me so,
Except he were deceiu'd as you are now.

Duke. This impudence shall not excuse your fault,
You are well knowne to be *Fallerio,*
The wicked husband of dead *Sostrata,*
And father to the vertuous *Alonso,*
And euen as sure as all these certeinties,
Thou didst contriue thy little Nephewes death.

Alen. True, for I am not false *Fallerio,*
Husband, nor father, as you do suggest,
And therefore did not hire the murtherers:
Which to be true acknowledge with your eyes.
                              Puls off his disguise.

Duke. How now my Lords, this is a myracle,
To shake off thirtie yeares so sodeinlie,
And turne from feeble age to flourishing youth.

Alb. But he my Lord that wrought this miracle,
Is not of power to free himselfe from death,
Through the performance of this suddaine change.

Duke. No, were he the chiefest hope of Christendome,
He should not liue for this presumption:
Vse no excuse, *Alenso* for thy life,
My doome of death shall be irreuocable.

Alen. Ill fare his soule, that would extenuate
The rigor of your life confounding doome:
I am prepar'd with all my hart to die,
For thats th'end of humaine miserie.

Duke. Then thus, you shall be hang'd immediatly,
For your illusion of the Magistrates,
With borrowed shapes of false antiquitie.

Alen. Thrice happy sentence, which I do imbrace,
With a more feruent and vnfained zeale,
Then an ambicious rule desiring man,
Would do a Iem bedecked Diadem,
Which brings more watchfull cares and discontent,
Then pompe, or honor, can remunerate:
When I am dead, let it be said of me,

                                        Alenso

2460

2470

2480

2490

Alenso died to set his father free.

Fal. That were a freedome worse then seruitude,
To cruell Turke, or damned Infidell :
Most righteous Iudge, I do appeale for Iustice,
Iustice on him that hath deserued death,
Not on *Alenso*, he is innocent.

  Alen. But I am guiltie of abbetting him,
Contrarie to his Maiesties Edict,
And therefore death is meritorious.

  Fall. I am the wretch that did subborne the slaues,
To murther poore *Pertillo* in the wood,
Spare, spare *Alenso*, he is innocent.

  Duke. What strange appeale is this, we know thee not,
None but *Fallerio* is accusde hereof.

  Alen. Then father get you hence, depart in time,
Least being knowne you suffer for the crime.

  Fal. Depart, and leaue thee clad in horrors cloake,
And suffer death for true affection :
Although my soule be guiltie of more sinne,
Then euer sinfull soule were guiltie of :
Yet fiends of hell would neuer suffer this,
I am thy father, though vnworthy so :
Oh still I see these weedes do seare your eyes :
I am *Fallerio*, make no doubt of me.   *Put off.*
Though thus disguisde, in habite, countenance,
Only to scape the terror of the lawe.

  Alen. And I *Alenso* that did succour him,
Gainst your commaundement, mightie Soueraigne:
Ponder your oath, your vowe, as God did liue,
I should not liue, if I did rescue him :
I did, God liues, and will reuenge it home,
If you defer my condigne punishment.

  Duke. Assure your selues you both shall suffer death:
But for *Fallerio*, he shall hang in chaines,
After he's dead, for he was principall.

  Fall. Vnsauerie Woormewood, Hemlock, bitter gall,
Brings no such bad, vnrelisht, sower taste,

Vnto

Vnto the tongue, as this death boding voice,
Brings to the eares of poore *Fallerio*.
Not for my selfe but for *Allensoes* sake,
Whome I haue murthered by my trechery:
Ah my dread Lord, if any little sparke,
Of melting pittie doth remaine aliue,
And not extinguisht by my impious deedes,
Oh kindle it vnto a happie flame,
To light *Allenso* from this miserie;
Which through dim death he's like to fall into.

   Allen. That were to ouerthrow my soule and all,
Should you reuerse this sentence of my death:
My selfe would play the death man on my selfe,
And ouertake your swift and winged soule,
Ere churlish *Caron* had transported you,
Vnto the fields of sad *Proserpina*.

   Duke. Cease, cease *Fallerio*, in thy bootlesse prayers,
I am resolu'd, I am inexorable,
Vesuuio, see their iudgement be performde,
And vse *Alenso* with all clemencie:
Prouided that the lawe be satisfied.

                Exit Duke and Alberto.
   Vesu. It shall be done with all respectiuenesse,
Haue you no donbt of that my gratious Lord.

   Fal. Here is a mercie mixt with equitie,
To shew him fauour, but cut off his head.

   Alen. My reuerend father, pacifie your selfe,
I can, and will, indure the stroake of death,
Were his appearance nere so horrible,
To meete *Pertillo* in another world.

   Fal. Thou shouldst haue tarried vntill natures course
Had beene extinct, that thou oregrowne with age,
Mightst die the death of thy progenitors,
Twas not thy meanes he died so soddenly,
But mine, that causing his, haue murthred thee.

   Alen. But yet I slew my mother, did I not?

   Fal. I, with reporting of my villanie,

                         The

The very audit of my wickednesse,
Had force enough to giue a sodaine death:
Ah sister, sister, now I call to minde,
Thy dying wordes now prou'd a prophesie,
If you deale ill with this distressed childe:
God will no doubt reuenge the innocent,
I haue delt ill, and God hath tane reuenge.

Allen. Now let vs leaue remembrance of past deedes,
And thinke on that which more concerneth vs.

Fal. With all my hart thou euer wert the spur,
Which prickt me on to any godlinesse:
And now thou doest indeuor to incite,
Me make my parting peace with God and men:
I doe confesse euen from my verie soule,
My hainous sinne and grieuous wickednesse,
Against my maker manie thousand waies:
Ab imo cordis I repent my selfe,
Of all my sinnes against his maiestie:
And heauenly father lay not to my charge,
The death of poore *Pertillo* and those men,
Which I suborn'd to be his murtherers,
When I appeare before thy heauenlie throne,
To haue my sentence, or of life or death.

Vesu. Amen, amen, and God continue still,
These mercie mouing meditations.

Allen. And thou great God which art omnipotent,
Powerfull enough for to redeeme our soules:
Euen from the verie gates of gaping hell,
Forgiue our sinnes, and wash away our faults;
In the sweete riuer of that precious blood,
Which thy deare sonne did shed in *Galgotha,*
For the remission of all contrite soules.

Fal. Forgiue thy death my thrice beloued sonne.

Allen. I doe, and father pardon my misdeedes,
Of disobedience and vnthankfullnesse.

Fal. Thou neuer yet wert disobedient,
Vnlesse I did commaund vnlawfulnesse,

K   Vn-

Vngratefulnesse did neuer trouble thee,
Thou art too bounteous thus to guerdon me.

   Allen. Come let vs kisse and thus imbrace in death,   2610
Euen when you will come bring vs to the place:
Where we may consumate our wretched nesse,
And change it for eternall hapinesse.   *Exeunt omnes.*

   Enter Merry *and* Rachel *to execution with Offi-*
cers with Halberdes , the Hangman
with a lather, &c.

   Mer. Now sister *Rachell* is the houre come,
Wherein we both must satisfie the law,
For *Beeches* death and harmelesse *Winchester:*
Weepe not sweete sister, for that cannot helpe,   2620
I doe confesse fore all this company,
That thou wert neuer priuie to their deathes,
But onelie helpest me when the deede was done,
To wipe the blood and hide away my sinne,
And since this fault hath brought thee to this shame,
I doe intreate thee on my bended knee,
To pardon me for thus offending thee.

   Rach. I doe forgiue you from my verie soule,
And thinke not that I shed these store of teares,
For that I price my life, or feare to dye,   2630
Though I confesse the manner of my death,
Is much more grieueuous then my death it selfe;
But I lament for that it hath beene said,
I was the author of this crueltie,
And did produce you to this wicked deede,
Whereof God knowes that I am innocent.

   Mer. Indeed thou art, thy conscience is at peace,   *Goe vp*
And feeles no terror for such wickednesse,   *the lather.*
Mine hath beene vexed but is now at rest,
For that I am assur'd my hainous sinne: 2640
Shall neuer rise in iudgement gainst my soule,
But that the blood of Iesus Christ hath power,

                                         To

To make my purple finne as white as Snowe.
One thing good people, witneffe here with me,
That I do dye in perfect charitie,
And do forgiue, as I would be forgiuen,
Firft of my God, and then of all the world:
Ceafe publifhing that I haue beene a man,
Train'd vp in murther, or in crueltie,
For fore this time, this time is all too foone,
I neuer flue or did confent to kill,
So helpe me God as this I fpeake is true:
I could fay something of my innocence,
In fornication and adulterie,
But I confeffe the iufteft man aliue
That beares about the frailtie of a man,
Cannot excufe himfelfe from daily finne,
In thought, in word, and deed, fuch was my life,
I neuer hated *Beech* in all my life,
Onely defire of money which he had,
And the inciting of that foe of man,
That greedie gulfe, that great *Lauiathan*,
Did halle me on to thefe callamities,
For which, euen now my very foule dooth bleede:
God ftrengthen me with patience to endure,
This chaftifement, which I confeffe too fmall
A punifhment for this my hainous finne:
Oh be couragious fifter, fight it well,
We fhall be crown'd with immortallitie.

 Rach. I will not faint, but combat manfully,
Chrift is of power to helpe and ftrengthen me.

 Officer. I pray make haft, the hower is almoft paft.

 Mer. I am prepar'd, oh God receiue my foule,
Forgiue my finnes, for they are numberleffe,
Receiue me God, for now I come to thee.

   Turne of the Lather: Rachel *fhrinketh.*

 Offi. Nay fhrinke not woman, haue a cheerefull heart.

 Rach. I, fo I do, and yet this finfull flefh,
Will be rebellious gainft my willing fpirit.

   K 2   Come

Come let me clime these steps that lead to heauen,   2680
Although they seeme the staires of infamie:
Let me be merror to ensuing times,
And teach all sisters how they do conceale,
The wicked deeds, of brethren, or of friends,
I not repent me of my loue to him,
But that thereby I haue prouoked God,
To heauie wrath and indignation,
Which turne away great God, for Christes sake.
Ah *Harry Williams*, thou wert chiefest cause,
That I do drinke of this most bitter cup,   2690
For hadst thou opened *Beeches* death at first,
The boy had liu'd, and thou hadst sau'd my life:
But thou art bronded with a marke of shame,
And I forgiue thee from my very soule,
Let him and me, learne all that heare of this,
To vtter brothers or their maisters misse,
Conceale no murther, least it do beget,
More bloody deeds of like deformitie.
Thus God forgiue my sinnes, receiue my soule,
And though my dinner be of bitter death,   2700
I hope my soule shall sup with Iesus Christ,
And see his presence euerlastingly.   *Dyeth.*

   Offi. The Lord of heauen haue mercy on her soule,
And teach all other by this spectacle,
To shunne such dangers as she ran into,
By her misguided taciturnitie:
Cut downe their bodies, giue hers funerall,
But let his body be conueyed hence,
To Mile-end greene, and there be hang'd in chaines.
                         Exeunt omnes.   2710

             Enter Truthe.

   Tru. See here the end of lucre and desire
Of riches, gotten by vnlawfull meanes,
What monstrous euils this hath brought to passe,
Your scarce drie eyes giue testimoniall,

                         The

The father, sonne; the sister, brother brings,
To open scandall, and contemptuous death.
   Enter Homicide and Couetousnesse.
But heere come they that wrought these deeds of ruthe,
As if they meant to plot new wickednesse :
Whether so fast, you damned miscreants?
Yee vaine deluders of the credulous,
That seeke to traine men to destruction.
 Mur. Why we will on, to set more harmes a flote,
That I may swim in riuers of warme blood,
Out-flowing from the sides of Innocents.
 Coue. I will intice the greedie minded soule,
To pull the fruite from the forbidden tree:
Yet *Tantall* like, he shall but glut his eye,
Nor feede his body with salubrious fruite,
 Tru. Hence Stigmaticks, you shall not harbor heare,
To practice execrable butcheries:
My selfe will bring your close designes to light,
And ouerthrow your vilde conspiracies,
No hart shall intertaine a murthrous thought,
Within the sea imbracing continent,
Where faire *Eliza* Prince of pietie,
Doth weare the peace adorned Diadem.
 Coue. Mauger the worst, I will haue many harts,
That shall affect my secret whisperings,
The chinck of golde is such a pleasing crie,
That all men wish to heare such harmony,
And I will place sterne murther by my side,
That we may do more harmes then haughty pride.
 Homi. Truth, now farewell, hereafter thou shalt see,
Ile vexe thee more with many tragedies.
 Truth. The more the pitty, would the hart of man,
Were not so open wide to entertaine,
The harmfull baites, of selfe deuouring sinne,
But from the first vnto the latter times,
It hath and will be so eternally,
Now it remaines to haue your good aduice,
     K 3   Vnto

Vnto a motion of some consequence,
There is a Barke thats newly rigd for sea,
Vnmand, vnfurnishd with munition:
She must incounter with a greater foe,
Then great *Alcydes* slue in *Lerna* Lake,
Would you be pleasd to man this willing barke,
With good conceits of her intencion,
To store her with the thundring furniture, 2760
Of smoothest smiles, and pleasing plaudiats,
She shall be able to endure the shock,
Of snarling *Zoylus*, and his cursed crue,
That seekes to sincke her in reproches waues,
And may perchance obteine a victorie,
Gainst curious carpes, and fawning Parasites:
But if you suffer her for want of ayde,
To be orewhelmd by her insulting foes,
Oh then she sinckes, that meant to passe the flood,
With stronger force to do her countrie good: 2770
It resteth thus whether she liue or dye,
She is your Beades-man euerlastinglie.

FINIS. Rob. Yarington.

Laus Deo.